Slow Cooker Favorites

BEEF

150+ EASY, DELICIOUS SLOW COOKER RECIPES,
from Meatloaf and Pot Roast to Beef Stroganoff

Adams Media
New York London Toronto Sydney New Delhi

Adamsmedia

Adams Media
An Imprint of Simon & Schuster, Inc.
57 Littlefield Street
Avon, Massachusetts 02322

First Adams Media trade paperback edition
JANUARY 2018

ADAMS MEDIA and colophon are trademarks of
Simon and Schuster.

For information about special discounts for bulk
purchases, please contact Simon & Schuster
Special Sales at 1-866-506-1949 or business@
simonandschuster.com.

The Simon & Schuster Speakers Bureau can bring
authors to your live event. For more information
or to book an event contact the Simon & Schuster
Speakers Bureau at 1-866-248-3049 or visit our
website at www.simonspeakers.com.

Interior design by Katrina Machado

Manufactured in the United States of America

10 9 8 7 6 5 4 3 2 1

Library of Congress Cataloging-in-Publication Data
Adams Media, firm.
Slow cooker favorites: beef / Adams Media.
Avon, Massachusetts: Adams Media, 2018.
Series: Slow Cooker Favorites.
Includes index.
LCCN 2017035852 (print) | LCCN 2017045393
(ebook) | ISBN 9781507206386 (pb) | ISBN
9781507206393 (ebook)
LCSH: Cooking (Beef) | Electric cooking, Slow. |
LCGFT: Cookbooks.
LCC TX749.5.B43 (ebook) | LCC TX749.5.B43 .S58
2017 (print) | DDC 641.6/62--dc23
LC record available at https://lccn.loc.gov/2017035852

ISBN 978-1-5072-0638-6
ISBN 978-1-5072-0639-3 (ebook)

Always follow safety and commonsense cooking
protocols while using kitchen utensils, operating
ovens and stoves, and handling uncooked food. If
children are assisting in the preparation of any recipe, they should always be supervised by an adult.

Contains material adapted from the following
titles published by Adams Media, an Imprint of
Simon & Schuster, Inc.: *The Everything® Paleolithic
Diet Slow Cooker Cookbook* by Emily Dionne,
copyright © 2013, ISBN 978-1-4405-5536-7; *The
Everything® Healthy Slow Cooker Cookbook* by
Rachel Rappaport with B.E. Horton, copyright ©
2010, ISBN 978-1-4405-0231-6; *The Everything®
One-Pot Cookbook* by Pamela Rice Hahn,
copyright © 2009, ISBN 978-1-59869-836-
7; *The Everything® Potluck Cookbook* by Linda
Larsen, copyright © 2009, ISBN 978-1-59869-990-
6; *The Everything® Weeknight Paleo Cookbook*
by Michelle Fagone, copyright © 2014, ISBN
978-1-4405-7229-6; *The Everything® Kosher Slow
Cooker Cookbook* by Dena G. Price, copyright ©
2012, ISBN 978-1-4405-4350-0; *The Everything®
Slow Cooker Cookbook, 2nd Edition* by Pamela
Rice Hahn, copyright © 2009, ISBN 978-1-59869-
977-7; *The Everything® Gluten-Free Slow Cooker
Cookbook* by Carrie S. Forbes, copyright © 2012,
ISBN 978-1-4405-3366-2; and *The Everything®
Slow Cooking for a Crowd Cookbook* by Katie
Thompson, copyright © 2005, ISBN 978-1-59337-
391-7.

Contents

Introduction

Are you sick of cleaning up a mountain of dirty dishes? Looking to serve a crowd? Does the simple act of eating a home-cooked meal seem like a luxury?

If this sounds familiar, it's time for you to plug in your slow cooker and make a hot meal a priority—not a chore.

With a slow cooker you can create everything from appetizers to soups and stews to flavorful entrées, and you don't have to worry about spending hours—or much time at all—in the kitchen. Just drop in your ingredients, turn on the slow cooker, and you're out the door with a delicious dinner guaranteed to greet you when you get home.

In *Slow Cooker Favorites: Beef*, you'll find more than 150 warming slow cooker recipes that make dinnertime easy, inexpensive, and incredibly versatile. These flavor-packed dishes come from a variety of cuisines— Mediterranean, Italian, Asian—and even include a number of American favorites like Texas Firehouse Chili, Yankee Pot Roast, and Basic Beef Stew. You'll also find a chapter that gives you the rundown on how to use, clean, and store your slow cooker and information on how to customize your recipes once you get the hang of using this appliance.

So whether you're craving Barbecue Meatballs, Meatloaf-Stuffed Green Peppers, Herbed Pot Roast, or just some Country Hamburger Casserole, with *Slow Cooker Favorites: Beef*, you'll always know what's for dinner.

CHAPTER 1

Slow Cooker Basics

So you know you want to use a slow cooker and you're excited to whip up the delicious beef dishes found throughout the book. But where do you start? In this chapter you'll learn everything you need to know to choose, cook with, clean, and store your slow cooker. In addition you'll find some basic techniques for using this appliance, as well as some info on the methods and terminology used in the book to make cooking with your slow cooker as easy as possible. Let's get cooking!

What Slow Cooker Equipment Should You Buy?

Maybe you've gone to buy a slow cooker and were overwhelmed by all the options. It can be intimidating. With so many different styles from which to choose, how do you pick the one that's right for you?

There are small 1-quart versions that are perfect for hot-dip appetizers and large 8-quart models that make enough stew for a large family. There are versions with automatic timers and warming settings. Some have removable crockery inserts, while others have the crock built into the device.

The first thing you need to do is take a look at how you'll be using the device. Are you routinely gone for more than nine hours during the day? If so, you might want to consider the automatic timer and warming functions because even a slow cooker can overcook some food. Do you want to make entire meals? The two-compartment model would provide more options. If you don't like to spend a lot of time washing pots and pans, consider a slow cooker with a removable crockery insert. These can be cleaned in the dishwasher, while self-contained units must be sponge cleaned. The good news is that a slow cooker remains a slow cooker. It's a relatively simple device that's hard to use incorrectly.

If you are lucky enough to plan your purchase of a slow cooker, define what you will be using it for. Do you have more than four people in your family? If so, you might want to go with a 6-quart or even 8-quart version. Someone who does a lot of entertaining or likes to freeze leftovers might want the larger version. Many of the recipes throughout this book call for either a 4- or a 6-quart slow cooker, so keep that in mind while choosing your appliance. Once you decide what type of slow cooker to buy, you'll need to figure out how to use it. Read on…

How to Use Your Slow Cooker

Today's slow cookers usually have two settings—high and low. The low setting is equivalent to about 200°F at its highest, while the high setting gets up to about 300°F. However, the reason they are listed as high and low is because the actual degrees don't matter. Since the food heats indirectly, absorbing the heat from the crockery, it will cook the same way within a 50-degree temperature range.

Slow cookers heat up slowly, usually taking two to three hours to get up to their highest temperature. This ensures that the food retains its nutrients while also preventing scorching or burning. It's also the reason you don't need to be home while the meal cooks. When your slow cooker is on, resist the urge to lift the cover to view, smell, or stir the contents. Every time you lift the cover of the slow cooker, valuable steam escapes, reducing the internal temperature several degrees. This steam that the slow cooker creates is an important factor in creating those marvelous flavors—foods are cooked in their own steam, literally infusing the flavor back in through the cooking process. This keeps the food moist and works to tenderize the meat and even the most stubborn vegetables. Every time you lift the cover, plan to add at least twenty minutes to your cooking time.

Slow Cooker Suggestions

The heating elements for a slow cooker are across the bottom of the slow cooker and up the sides. Until you become very familiar with the quirks of your slow cooker, cooking on low is the safest bet for ensuring the food turns out the way you want it.

Even the most inexperienced cook can quickly master slow cooker recipes. Just keep the following things in mind:

- Cut meat and vegetables to the same size to ensure even cooking in soups and stews.
- Place slow-cooking items such as hard vegetables—rutabagas, turnips, potatoes—on the bottom of the slow cooker.
- Slow cooker recipes don't like water. Because the food is infused with steam, very little water escapes. When converting a recipe from a regular cookbook, use about half the water and add more during the last hour of the cooking cycle if necessary.

- Most traditional slow cooker recipes take seven to nine hours on the low setting. The high setting takes about half that time but doesn't tenderize the meat as much.
- Spices and aromatic vegetables have different characteristics when slow cooked. Some, such as green peppers and bay leaves, increase in intensity when slow cooked. Others, such as onions and cinnamon, tend to lose flavor over the long cooking process. Most slow cooker recipes reflect this difference, although you may have to adjust for your own tastes.
- When cooking traditional slow cooker meals such as soups, stews, and meats, make sure the slow cooker is at least half full and the food does not extend beyond 1" below the top. This ensures even cooking.
- Don't thaw food in the slow cooker. While it may seem a natural use, frozen food actually heats up too slowly to effectively prevent bacterial growth when in a slow cooker. It's better to thaw food overnight in a refrigerator or use the microwave.

With these things in mind, you'll be a slow cooker professional before you know it.

How to Care for Your Slow Cooker

Slow cookers are very simple appliances. However, they do need some special care. If you follow these rules, your slow cooker will produce healthy meals for many years:

- Never, never, never immerse the slow cooker in water. If it's plugged in at the time, you could receive a shock. If it isn't plugged in, you could damage the heating element.
- Always check for nicks or cuts in the electrical cord before plugging it into the outlet. This is especially important because you may be leaving the slow cooker on for several hours with no one in the house.
- Parts of the slow cooker can be cleaned in a dishwasher. If you have a removable crockery core, place it on the bottom rack. If you have a

plastic cover, be sure to place it in the top rack of the dishwasher so it doesn't warp. If the crockery container isn't removable, simply use a soft cloth or sponge to wash it out. Always use a damp cloth to wash the metal housing.

- Remove baked-on food from the crockery container with a nonabrasive cleaner and a damp sponge. Do not scrub with abrasives, as these can scratch the crock, creating areas for bacteria to reside.

Be sure to follow all of these rules to guarantee your slow cooker will both last for many years and perform at maximum potential with each use.

Slow Cooker Suggestions

Cooking with a slow cooker becomes even easier when you use slow cooker liners. The liners are made of food-safe, heat-resistant nylon. They also make slow cooker cleanup fast and easy because you simply place the liner in the slow cooker crock, add the ingredients, cook according to the recipe instructions, throw the liner away when you're done, and wipe down the slow cooker and wash the lid.

What Else Do You Need to Know?

So now you know how to buy, cook with, and clean your slow cooker. Now let's take a look at what else you need to know to successfully make the deliciously easy meals found throughout the following recipe chapters.

Learn Some Cooking Terms

Throughout this book you'll encounter cooking terms usually associated with other methods of cooking. While the slow cooker does provide an easy way to cook foods, there are simple tricks you can use to let your slow cooker mimic those other methods. Cooking method terms you'll find in this book include the following:

- **Baking** usually involves putting food that's in a baking pan or oven-proof casserole dish in a preheated oven; the food cooks by being surrounded by the hot, dry air of your oven. (In the case of a convection oven, it cooks by being surrounded by circulating hot, dry air.) In the slow cooker, food can be steam-baked in the cooker itself, or you can mimic the effect of baking at a low oven temperature by putting the food in a baking dish and resting that dish on a cooking insert or rack.

- **Braising** usually starts by browning meat in a skillet on top of the stove and then putting the meat with a small amount of liquid in a pan with a lid or covering and slowly cooking it. Braising can take place on the stovetop, in the oven, or in a slow cooker. The slow-cooking process tenderizes the meat. Incidentally, the liquid that's in the pan after you've braised meat often can be used to make a flavorful sauce or gravy.

- **Sautéing** is the method of quickly cooking small or thin pieces of food in some oil or butter that has been brought to temperature in a sauté pan over medium to medium-high heat. Alternatively, you can sauté in a good-quality nonstick pan without using added fat; instead use a little broth, nonstick cooking spray, or water in place of the oil or butter. As mentioned later in this chapter, another alternative is to steam-sauté food in the microwave.

- **Stewing** is similar to braising in that food is slowly cooked in a liquid; however, stewing involves a larger liquid-to-food ratio. In other words, you use far more liquid when you're stewing food. It is the method often associated with recipes for the slow cooker. Not surprisingly, this method is most often used to make stew.

Make Each Dish Your Own

Throughout this book you'll find suggestions for how you can take shortcuts or add a bit of additional personality to a dish without compromising the recipe. Straying from the recipe may seem scary at first, but once you understand the logic behind such shortcuts, you'll begin to look at them as alternative measures rather than total improvisations. Before you know it, you'll be adding a little bit of this and a little bit of that with the best of them. For example:

- **Use broth bases or homemade broth:** Use of a broth base or home-made broth lets you eliminate the need to stir-fry meat and sauté vegetables. In addition, broth bases can be made double strength, which saves you the time of reducing broth, and you avoid that briny, overly salty taste associated with bouillon cubes. Bases also take up less storage space. It usually only takes ¾ to 1 teaspoon of broth mixed together with a cup of water to make 1 cup of broth. A 16-ounce container of base, for example, is enough to make 6 gallons of broth.

- **Use a microwave-safe measuring cup:** Rather than dirtying a microwave-safe bowl and a measuring cup, planning the steps so that you add the ingredients to a microwave-safe measuring cup means you can use it to sauté or steam onions or other vegetables called for in the recipe. This makes it easier to pour the results into the slow cooker, and you end up with fewer dishes to wash.

- **Steam-sauté vegetables in the microwave:** Sautéing vegetables in the microwave has the added advantage of using less oil than it would take to sauté them in a pan. Or you can compromise further and eliminate the oil entirely and substitute broth if you prefer. Just because a recipe suggests sautéing the onions in a nonstick skillet doesn't mean that you can't use the alternative microwave method, or vice versa. Use the method that is most convenient for you. On the other hand, skipping other steps, like sautéing onion, carrot, celery, or bell pepper before you add them to the slow cooker, won't ruin the taste of the food; you'll just end up with a dish that tastes good instead of great. When time is an issue, there may be times when good is good enough. And that's okay.

- **Take advantage of ways to enhance or correct the flavor:** Like salt, a little bit of sugar can act as a flavor enhancer. The sweetness of sugar, honey, applesauce, or jelly can also be used to help tame an overly hot, spicy dish or curry. Just start out adding a little bit at a time; you want to adjust the flavor without overcorrecting, which could create a dish with a cloying result.

- **Use fresh herbs:** There are other times you may need to adjust some of the recipe instructions. For example, if you have fresh herbs on hand, it's almost always better to use those instead of dried seasoning;

however, if you substitute fresh herbs, don't add them until near the end of the cooking time. Also keep in mind that you need to use three times the amount called for in the recipe. In other words, if the recipe specifies 1 teaspoon of dried thyme, you'd add 1 tablespoon (3 teaspoons) of fresh thyme.

- **Use frozen, not fresh:** If you're using frozen meat to replace the raw meat called for in the recipe, chances are you can add it straight from the freezer to the slow cooker and not greatly affect the cooking time. If the meat is thawed, you'll want to wait until near the end of the cooking time to add it so that you don't overcook the meat.

Again, if you're nervous or just aren't comfortable cooking with a slow cooker yet, don't worry. Follow the recipes throughout the book, learn what you like and what you don't like, and then take the next step. The possibilities are endless!

CHAPTER 2

Soups and Stews

Greek Meatball Soup

1 pound lean ground beef

¼ pound ground pork

1 small onion, peeled and minced

1 clove garlic, peeled and minced

6 tablespoons uncooked converted long-grain white rice

1 tablespoon dried parsley

2 teaspoons dried dill or mint

1 teaspoon dried oregano

¼ teaspoon salt

¼ teaspoon freshly ground black pepper

3 large eggs, divided

6 cups chicken or vegetable broth, or water, divided

1 medium onion, peeled and chopped

1 cup baby carrots, each sliced into thirds

2 large potatoes, peeled and cut into cubes

1 celery stalk, finely chopped

2 tablespoons masa harina (corn flour)

⅓ cup fresh lemon juice

1. In a large bowl mix the meat, minced onion, garlic, rice, parsley, dill or mint, oregano, salt, pepper, and 1 egg. Shape into small meatballs and set aside.

2. Add 2 cups broth or water to the slow cooker. Add the meatballs, chopped onion, carrots, potatoes, and celery and then pour in enough broth or water to cover the meatballs and vegetables. Cover and cook on low for 6 hours.

3. In a small bowl or measuring cup beat the 2 remaining eggs and then whisk in the corn flour. Gradually whisk in the lemon juice and then ladle in about a cup of the hot broth from the slow cooker, doing so in a slow, steady stream, beating continuously until all of the hot liquid has been incorporated into the egg–corn flour mixture.

4. Stir this mixture into the slow cooker, being careful not to break the meatballs. Continue to cook on low for 1 hour or until mixture is thickened.

Beef-Vegetable Soup

7 large carrots, peeled, 1 grated and 6 diced

2 celery stalks, finely diced

1 large sweet onion, peeled and diced

8 ounces fresh mushrooms, cleaned and sliced

1 tablespoon extra-virgin olive oil

1 teaspoon butter, melted

1 clove garlic, peeled and minced

4 cups beef broth

6 medium potatoes, peeled and diced

1 tablespoon dried parsley

¼ teaspoon dried oregano

¼ teaspoon dried rosemary

1 bay leaf

¼ teaspoon salt

¼ teaspoon freshly ground black pepper

1 (3-pound) chuck roast, trimmed of fat and cut into bite-sized pieces

1 (10-ounce) package frozen green beans, thawed

1 (10-ounce) package frozen whole kernel corn, thawed

1 (10-ounce) package frozen baby peas, thawed

Fresh parsley

1. Add the grated carrot, celery, onion, mushrooms, oil, and butter to the slow cooker. Stir to coat the vegetables in the oil and butter. Cover and cook on high for 30 minutes or until the vegetables are soft.

2. Stir in the garlic. Add the broth, diced carrots, potatoes, dried parsley, oregano, rosemary, bay leaf, salt, pepper, and beef to the slow cooker. Cover and cook on low for 6 hours or until the beef is tender and the potatoes are cooked through.

3. Remove and discard the bay leaf. Stir in the green beans, corn, and peas; cover and cook on low for 1 hour or until the vegetables are heated through. Taste for seasoning and add additional salt, pepper, and herbs if needed. Garnish with parsley.

Slow Cooker Suggestions

Make Beef-Vegetable Soup a tomato-based dish by substituting 2 (15-ounce) cans of diced tomatoes for the beef broth.

Barbecue Beef and Bean Soup

1 pound great northern beans, soaked

1 large onion, peeled and diced

1/8 teaspoon plus 1/4 teaspoon freshly ground black pepper, divided

2 pounds beef short or Western ribs

6 cups water

3/4 cup barbecue sauce

1/4 teaspoon salt

1 tablespoon brown sugar

1. Rinse and drain the beans and add them to a bowl or saucepan. Add enough water to cover the beans by 2". Cover and let soak overnight or for 8 hours.

2. Drain the beans, then rinse and drain again.

3. Add enough water to cover the beans by 2" in a saucepan. Bring to a boil over high heat, and then reduce the heat and simmer the beans for 40 minutes to 1 hour or until they just begin to become tender. Drain.

4. Once the beans are precooked, add them to the slow cooker. Stir in the onion and 1/8 teaspoon pepper. Add the beef ribs and pour in the water. Cover and cook on low for 8 hours or until the beans are cooked through.

5. Remove the short ribs and cut the meat from the bones. Stir the meat and barbecue sauce into the beans. Cover and cook on low for 1 hour. Taste for seasoning and add 1/4 teaspoon salt, 1/4 teaspoon pepper, and brown sugar.

Slow-Cooked Hearty Beef and Cabbage Soup

¼ pound Easy Slow-Cooked "Roast" Beef (see Chapter 5)

1 small head cabbage, chopped

1 medium white or yellow onion, peeled and chopped

2 large carrots, peeled and thinly sliced

¼ cup uncooked long-grain brown rice

2 celery stalks, sliced into ½" pieces

1 clove garlic, peeled and minced

3 cups nonfat, low-salt beef broth

2 (14.5-ounce) cans Muir Glen Organic Diced Tomatoes No-Salt-Added

½ cup water

¼ teaspoon granulated sugar

⅛ teaspoon freshly ground black pepper

1. Add the cooked beef to the slow cooker. Mix together all the remaining ingredients in a large bowl and then pour over the beef.

2. Set the slow cooker on high until the mixture begins to boil. Reduce heat to low and simmer for 8–10 hours. Adjust seasonings if necessary.

Italian Wedding Soup

1 pound frozen meatballs, thawed

6 cups chicken broth

1 pound curly endive or escarole, coarsely chopped

2 large eggs

2 tablespoons freshly grated Parmigiano-Reggiano cheese

¼ teaspoon salt

¼ teaspoon freshly ground black pepper

1. Add the meatballs, broth, and endive or escarole to the slow cooker; cover and cook on low for 4 hours. Use a slotted spoon to remove the meatballs to a serving bowl; cover and keep warm. Increase the setting of the slow cooker to high; cook uncovered while you whisk the eggs.

2. Add the eggs, cheese, salt, and pepper to a small bowl; whisk to blend. Stir the soup in the slow cooker in a circular motion and then drizzle the egg mixture into the moving broth. Use a fork to separate the eggs into thin strands. Once the eggs are set, pour the soup over the meatballs.

Slow Cooker Suggestions

Wedding soup consists of some sort of greens (endive, escarole, cabbage, lettuce, kale, or spinach) and meat served in a broth. Mix and match different greens and meats to get a wedding soup that suits your unique taste.

Pho

1 tablespoon coriander seeds

1 tablespoon whole cloves

6 star anise

1 cinnamon stick

1 tablespoon fennel seed

1 tablespoon whole cardamom

4" knob fresh gingerroot, sliced

1 medium onion, sliced

Water as needed

3 pounds beef knuckles

1 quart beef stock

¾ pound thinly sliced lean beef

8 ounces Vietnamese rice noodles

½ cup chopped cilantro

½ cup chopped Thai basil

2 cups mung bean sprouts

1. In a large, dry nonstick skillet over medium-high heat, cook the spices, ginger, and onion until the seeds start to pop. The onion and ginger should look slightly caramelized. Place spices, ginger, and onion in a cheesecloth packet and tie it securely.

2. Fill a large pot with water. Bring the water to a boil and add the beef knuckles. Boil for 10 minutes. Remove from the heat and skim off the foam that rises to the surface.

3. Place the bones and the cheesecloth packet into a 6–7-quart slow cooker. Add the stock and fill the slow cooker with water, leaving 1" of headroom. Cook on low for up to 10 hours or overnight. Strain off any solids. Remove the bones and the packet.

4. Add the sliced beef and noodles. Cook on low for 15 minutes or until the beef is cooked and the noodles are tender. Arrange cilantro, basil, and bean sprouts on top.

Vietnamese Beef Noodle Soup

1 (3-pound) English-cut chuck roast, trimmed of fat
and cut into bite-sized pieces

3 medium yellow onions, peeled, 2 quartered, 1 sliced paper-thin

1 (4") piece (about 4 ounces) fresh gingerroot,
cut into 1" pieces

5 star anise

6 whole cloves

1 (3") cinnamon stick

¼ teaspoon salt

2 cups beef broth

Water

½ pound small (⅛"-wide) dried or fresh *banh pho*
noodles ("rice sticks" or Thai *chantaboon*)

4 tablespoons fish sauce

1 tablespoon brown sugar

4 green onions, green part only, cut into thin rings

⅓ cup chopped fresh cilantro

¼ teaspoon freshly ground black pepper

1. Add the beef, quartered onions, ginger, star anise, cloves, cinnamon stick, salt, and broth to the slow cooker. Add enough water to cover the meat by about 1". Cook on low for 6 hours or until the beef is pull-apart tender.

2. About ½ hour before serving soak the onion slices in cold water. For dried rice noodles: cover them with hot water and allow to soak for 15–20 minutes or until softened and opaque white; drain in colander. For fresh rice noodles: untangle and place in a colander, then rinse briefly with cold water.

3. Remove the meat from the broth with a slotted spoon; shred the meat. Strain the broth through a fine strainer, discarding the spices and onion; return strained broth to the slow cooker along with the shredded meat.

4. Set the slow cooker on the high setting to bring the meat and broth to a boil.

5. Stir the fish sauce and brown sugar into the broth. (The broth should taste slightly too strong because the noodles and other ingredients are not salted. Therefore, to test for seasoning, you may want to taste the broth and meat with some noodles. If you desire a stronger, saltier flavor, add more fish sauce. Add more brown sugar to make the broth sweeter if desired. If the broth is already too salty, add some additional water to dilute it.)

6. Blanch the noodles in stages by adding as many noodles to a strainer as you can submerge in the boiling broth without causing the slow cooker to boil over. The noodles will collapse and lose their stiffness in about 15–20 seconds. At that time, pull strainer from the broth, letting the excess broth clinging to them drain back into cooker.

7. Empty noodles into bowls, allowing each serving to fill about ⅓ of the bowl, and then ladle hot broth and beef over the noodles. (If you're feeding a crowd and will be filling all bowls at the same time, you can stir the noodles into the broth, let them simmer for 15 seconds, and then immediately ladle the broth, beef, and noodles into the bowls.)

8. Garnish with onion slices, scallions, and chopped cilantro and finish with freshly ground black pepper.

Slow Cooker Suggestions

If desired, have these additional garnishes available at the table: sprigs of spearmint (*hung lui*), sprigs of Asian/Thai basil (*hung que*), thorny cilantro leaves (*ngo gai*), bean sprouts (about ½ pound), blanched and thinly sliced red hot chilies (such as Thai bird or dragon), and lime wedges.

Stuffed Pepper Soup

1½ pounds ground beef, browned and drained

3 cups diced green bell pepper

2 cups peeled and diced butternut squash

1 (28-ounce) can diced peeled tomatoes

1 (28-ounce) can tomato sauce

¾ cup raw honey

¼ teaspoon each dried seasonings of choice (basil, thyme, oregano, onion flakes, etc.)

1. Mix all the ingredients in a 4-quart slow cooker. Cover and cook on low for 3–4 hours or until the green peppers are cooked.
2. Turn heat to high and cook for 20–30 more minutes. Serve.

Vietnamese Cucumber Soup

2 quarts water

1 pound ground beef

6 tablespoons fish sauce, divided

⅛ teaspoon ground black pepper

4 large cucumbers, peeled, halved, seeded, and sliced

2 green onions, chopped

1. Add the water to a large pot (to be placed inside a large slow cooker) and bring to a simmer over medium-high heat.
2. In a large bowl combine the meat with 2 tablespoons fish sauce. Add the pepper and mix thoroughly.
3. Make meatballs out of the meat mixture and then transfer into boiling water along with the cucumber slices. Cook for 15 minutes; remove any foam and discard. Transfer the whole boiling pot into slow cooker.
4. Add the green onions and remaining 4 tablespoons fish sauce. Cover and cook on high for 1½–2 hours.

Slow Cooker Stroganoff Soup

1 (1½-pound) sirloin roast, trimmed of fat and
    cut into 1" cubes

1 teaspoon salt

⅛ teaspoon pepper

2 medium onions, peeled and chopped

4 cloves garlic, peeled and minced

1 bay leaf

1 teaspoon dried oregano

6 cups beef broth

2 cups water

2 cups sliced carrots

½ cup sour cream

¼ cup light cream

2 tablespoons flour

2 cups egg noodles

1. Place meat in 5–6-quart slow cooker; sprinkle with salt and pepper.
2. Add onions, garlic, bay leaf, and oregano and stir. Add beef broth, water, and carrots and cover. Cook on low for 8–9 hours.
3. Turn slow cooker to high. In small bowl combine sour cream, light cream, and flour and mix with wire whisk until smooth.
4. Stir egg noodles and sour cream mixture into slow cooker. Cover and cook on high for 15–20 minutes until noodles are tender and soup has thickened slightly. Stir well and serve.

Tuxedo Soup

SERVES
8

1 pound lean ground beef

1 medium onion, peeled and diced

1 small green pepper, seeded and diced

1 celery stalk, diced

1 medium carrot, peeled and diced

4 cloves garlic, peeled and minced

2 (15-ounce) cans diced tomatoes, undrained

1 cup water

1 (26-ounce) jar spaghetti sauce

1 tablespoon sugar

½ teaspoon dried Italian seasoning

Dash red pepper flakes

1 cup bowtie pasta

¼ teaspoon salt

¼ teaspoon freshly ground black pepper

½ cup grated Parmigiano-Reggiano or mozzarella cheese

¼ cup minced fresh flat-leaf parsley

1. Add the ground beef, onion, green pepper, celery, and carrot to a nonstick skillet and, stirring frequently, sauté over medium-high heat for 8 minutes or until the vegetables are tender and the meat is no longer pink. Stir in the garlic and sauté for 30 seconds. Drain and discard any excess fat. Transfer to the slow cooker.

2. Stir in the undrained tomatoes, water, spaghetti sauce, sugar, Italian seasoning, and red pepper flakes. Cover and cook on low for 8 hours.

3. Cook the pasta according to package directions. Drain and stir into the slow cooker. Thin the soup with additional hot water if necessary. Taste for seasoning and add salt and pepper if desired. Ladle into soup bowls. Sprinkle cheese over each serving. Garnish with parsley.

Slow Cooker Suggestions

Thanks to the spaghetti sauce, you can hide more vegetables in Tuxedo Soup and the kids won't even notice. For example, dice a few more carrots and stir them in with the other ingredients in Step 2.

Beef Stew with Root Vegetables and Raisins

SERVES
8

1 tablespoon vegetable oil

1 tablespoon butter, melted

1 large onion, peeled and diced

1 celery stalk, finely diced

2 tablespoons all-purpose flour

¼ teaspoon salt

¼ teaspoon freshly ground black pepper

1 (2-pound) chuck roast, trimmed of fat and cut into 1" cubes

1 (1-pound) bag baby carrots

2 large parsnips, peeled and diced

2 large Yukon gold or red potatoes, peeled and diced

2 (14.5-ounce) cans diced tomatoes, undrained

2 cups beef broth

2 cloves garlic, peeled and minced

1 bay leaf

1 teaspoon dried thyme

½ cup almond- or pimiento-stuffed green olives

⅓ cup golden raisins

1. Add the oil, butter, onion, and celery to the slow cooker. Cover and, stirring occasionally, cook on high for 30 minutes.

2. Place the flour, salt, and pepper in a plastic bag and add the meat cubes; close and shake to coat the meat. Add the meat to the slow cooker, stirring it into the onion and celery.

3. Add the carrots, parsnips, potatoes, tomatoes, broth, garlic, bay leaf, thyme, olives, and raisins to the cooker; stir to combine. Reduce the heat setting to low; cover and cook for 8 hours.

4. Remove and discard bay leaf. Serve warm.

Beef and Guinness Stew

2 teaspoons canola oil

1 large onion, peeled and diced

2 medium parsnips, peeled and diced

2 medium carrots, peeled and diced

2 celery stalks, diced

3 cloves garlic, peeled and minced

2 large russet potatoes, peeled and diced

2 tablespoons minced fresh rosemary

1 (2-pound) lean top round roast, cut into 1" cubes

1 tablespoon dark brown sugar

$\frac{1}{4}$ teaspoon salt

$\frac{1}{2}$ teaspoon freshly ground black pepper

1 tablespoon cocoa powder

1 cup water

$\frac{1}{2}$ cup Guinness Extra Stout

$\frac{1}{2}$ cup frozen peas

1. Heat the oil in a large skillet over medium heat. Sauté the onions, parsnip, carrots, celery, garlic, potatoes, rosemary, and beef until the ingredients begin to soften and brown. Drain any excess fat.
2. Add to a 4-quart slow cooker. Sprinkle with sugar, salt, pepper, and cocoa. Pour in the water and Guinness. Stir. Cook for 8–9 hours on low.
3. Add the frozen peas. Cover and cook an additional $\frac{1}{2}$ hour on high. Stir before serving.

Slow Cooker Suggestions

Leaner cuts like top round are excellent choices for slow cooking because the long cooking time tenderizes them. Look for cuts that have minimal marbling, and trim off any excess fat before cooking. Searing and sautéing are good ways to cook off some external fat before adding the meat to the slow cooker. Drain any excess fat.

Beef and Vegetable Stew

2 teaspoons canola oil

1 large onion, peeled and diced

2 medium parsnips, peeled and diced

2 large carrots, peeled and diced

2 celery stalks, diced

3 cloves garlic, peeled and minced

2 medium red potatoes, diced

1 tablespoon minced fresh tarragon

2 tablespoons minced fresh rosemary

1 (1-pound) lean top round roast, cut into 1" cubes

1/4 teaspoon salt

1/2 teaspoon freshly ground black pepper

1 1/2 cups water

1/2 cup frozen peas

1 fennel bulb, diced

1 tablespoon minced fresh parsley

1. Heat the oil in a large skillet over medium heat. Sauté the onion, parsnip, carrots, celery, garlic, potatoes, tarragon, rosemary, and beef until the ingredients begin to soften and brown. Drain off any excess fat.

2. Place the mixture into a 4-quart slow cooker. Sprinkle with salt and pepper. Pour in the water. Stir. Cook for 8–9 hours on low.

3. Add the frozen peas and fennel. Cover and cook an additional ½ hour on high. Stir in the parsley before serving.

Basic Beef Stew

Nonstick cooking spray

4 tablespoons vegetable oil

⅓ cup brown rice flour

1 tablespoon garlic powder

1 teaspoon salt

1 teaspoon freshly ground black pepper

1 (2-pound) chuck roast, trimmed of fat
and cut into 1" cubes

1 medium onion, peeled and diced

6 large potatoes, peeled and diced

6 medium carrots, peeled and sliced

3 celery stalks, sliced

4 cups gluten-free beef broth

1. Grease a 4- or 6-quart slow cooker with nonstick cooking spray. In a large skillet heat oil over medium-high heat.

2. In a zip-top plastic bag mix together the flour, garlic powder, salt, and pepper. Add a small handful of beef and shake until well coated. Repeat until all beef is coated in the flour mixture.

3. Brown beef in batches in hot oil, about 1 minute per side. Remove the browned meat and place in the slow cooker.

4. Lower heat under skillet to medium and add onions. Cook until softened, about 3–5 minutes, then place on top of beef in slow cooker.

5. Add remaining ingredients to slow cooker. Cover and cook on high for 4 hours or on low for 6–8 hours.

Tex-Mex Beef Stew

2 tablespoons extra-virgin olive or vegetable oil

1 (4-pound) English or chuck roast, trimmed of fat and cut into 1" cubes

1 (7-ounce) can green chilies

2 (15-ounce) cans diced tomatoes

1 (8-ounce) can tomato sauce

1 large sweet onion, peeled and diced

1 medium green bell pepper, seeded and diced

6 cloves garlic, peeled and minced

1 tablespoon ground cumin

1 teaspoon freshly ground black pepper

¼ teaspoon ground cayenne pepper

2 tablespoons lime juice

2 small jalapeño peppers, seeded and diced

Beef broth or water, as needed

1 bunch fresh cilantro, chopped

1. Add the oil to a large skillet over medium-high heat. Add the beef and stir-fry for 8 minutes or until it's well browned.

2. Add beef to a 6-quart slow cooker and stir in the chilies, tomatoes, tomato sauce, onion, bell pepper, garlic, cumin, black pepper, cayenne, lime juice, and jalapeño peppers. If needed, add enough beef broth or water so that all the ingredients in the cooker are covered by liquid.

3. Cover and cook on low for 9–10 hours.

4. Remove the lid and stir in the cilantro. Serve immediately.

Country Beef and Vegetable Stew

SERVES
8

2 celery stalks, diced

1 (3-pound) boneless chuck roast

1/4 teaspoon salt

1/4 teaspoon freshly ground black pepper

1 large onion, peeled and diced

2 cloves garlic, peeled and minced

2 cups beef broth

1/4 cup red wine vinegar

1 tablespoon Worcestershire sauce

1/2 teaspoon dried thyme

1 teaspoon dried marjoram

4 large potatoes, scrubbed and diced

2 medium turnips, scrubbed and diced

1 (2-pound) bag baby carrots

1 (1-pound) bag frozen pearl onions, thawed

1/4 cup butter, softened

1/4 cup all-purpose flour

1. Add the celery, roast, salt, pepper, onion, garlic, broth, vinegar, Worcestershire sauce, thyme, marjoram, potatoes, turnips, carrots, and pearl onions to the slow cooker.

2. Cover and cook on low for 8 hours or until the beef is tender and the vegetables are cooked through.

3. To thicken the pan juices, use a slotted spoon to transfer the meat and vegetables to a serving platter; cover and keep warm. Increase the temperature on the slow cooker to high. Skim and discard any fat from the pan juices.

4. In a small bowl use a fork to blend together the butter and flour, and then whisk about a cup of the pan juices into the butter and flour.

5. When the remaining pan juices begin to bubble around the edges, slowly whisk in the butter-flour mixture. Cook and stir for 10 minutes or until the mixture is thickened and the flour taste is cooked out of the sauce. Taste for seasoning and add salt and pepper if desired.

6. Carefully stir the cooked vegetables into the thickened sauce. Cut the meat into bite-sized pieces and fold into the sauce and vegetables.

7. Pour the thickened pan juices and vegetables into a tureen or serve directly from the slow cooker.

Slow Cooker Suggestions

Prepare a 12-ounce package of steam-in-the-bag frozen green beans according to package directions. When they're done, transfer them to a serving bowl and, before you've added the vegetables back into the thickened sauce in Step 2, mix some of the cooked potatoes, carrots, and pearl onions into the steamed beans. Dress the vegetables with red-wine vinaigrette. Season with salt and pepper to taste.

Beef and Sweet Potato Stew

¾ cup brown rice flour

1½ teaspoons salt, divided

1½ teaspoons ground black pepper, divided

1¼ pounds stew beef, cut into 1" chunks

¼ cup olive oil, divided

1 medium yellow onion, peeled and diced

2 cups diced carrots

¾ pound cremini mushrooms, cleaned and cut in half

6 cloves garlic, peeled and minced

3 tablespoons tomato paste

½ cup red wine

1 pound sweet potatoes, peeled and diced

4 cups beef broth

1 bay leaf

1½ teaspoons dried thyme

1 tablespoon gluten-free Worcestershire sauce

1 tablespoon sugar

1. In a large zip-top plastic bag place flour, 1 teaspoon salt, and 1 teaspoon pepper. Add beef and close the bag. Shake lightly and open bag and make sure that all of the beef is coated in flour and seasoning. Set aside.

2. In a large skillet heat 2 tablespoons olive oil over medium heat. Cook beef in small batches until browned on all sides, about 1 minute per side. Add beef to a greased 4–6-quart slow cooker.

3. In the same skillet heat the remaining 2 tablespoons olive oil. Add onion and carrots and cook until onions are translucent, about 5 minutes.

4. Add mushrooms and garlic and cook for another 2–3 minutes.

5. Add tomato paste and heat through. Deglaze the pan with the wine, scraping the stuck-on bits from the bottom of the pan. Add cooked vegetable mixture on top of the beef in the slow cooker.

6. Add the sweet potatoes, broth, bay leaf, thyme, and Worcestershire sauce. Cover and cook on low for 8 hours or on high for 4 hours.

7. Before serving add sugar and remaining salt and pepper.

Marsala Beef Stew

2 tablespoons extra-virgin olive oil

1 tablespoon butter

1 (2-pound) English-cut chuck roast, trimmed of fat and cut into bite-sized pieces

2 tablespoons all-purpose flour

1 small carrot, peeled and finely diced

1 celery stalk, finely diced

1 large yellow onion, peeled and diced

3 cloves garlic, peeled and minced

8 ounces mushrooms, cleaned and sliced

$\frac{1}{2}$ cup dry white wine

1 cup Marsala wine

$\frac{1}{2}$ teaspoon dried rosemary

$\frac{1}{2}$ teaspoon dried oregano

$\frac{1}{2}$ teaspoon dried basil

2 cups beef broth

2 cups water

$\frac{1}{4}$ teaspoon salt

$\frac{1}{4}$ teaspoon freshly ground black pepper

1. Add oil and butter to a large nonstick skillet over medium-high heat.

2. Put the beef pieces and flour in a large zip-top bag; close and toss to coat the meat in the flour. Add as many pieces of beef that will comfortably fit in the pan without crowding it and brown for 10 minutes or until the meat takes on a rich, dark outer color. Transfer the browned meat to the slow cooker.

3. Reduce the heat to medium and add the carrot and celery; sauté for 3–5 minutes or until soft. Add the onion and sauté until the onion is transparent. Add the garlic and sauté for an additional 30 seconds. Stir in the mushrooms; sauté until tender. Transfer the sautéed vegetables and mushrooms to the slow cooker.

continued on next page

4. Add the remaining flour-coated beef to the slow cooker; stir to mix.

5. Add the wines to the skillet and stir to pick up any browned bits sticking to the pan. Pour into the slow cooker. Add the rosemary, oregano, basil, broth, water, salt, and pepper to the slow cooker.

6. Cover and cook on low for 6–8 hours or until the meat is tender. (You may need to allow the stew to cook uncovered for an hour or so to evaporate any extra liquid to thicken the sauce.)

7. Taste for seasoning and add salt and pepper if needed. The taste of the stew will benefit if you allow it to rest uncovered off of the heat for a ½ hour and then put the crock back in the slow cooker over low heat long enough to bring it back to temperature, but that step isn't necessary; you can serve it immediately if you prefer.

Slow Cooker Suggestions

Searing meat does not seal in the juices. But it does intensify the flavor of a dish by adding another flavor dimension. Sautéing the vegetables and mushrooms adds flavor too. The stew will still be good if you simply coat the meat in flour and add it to the slow cooker along with all of the other ingredients, but it's better if you take the time to do the searing and sautéing suggested in Step 1.

Quick and Easy Stew

1 (2-pound) chuck roast, trimmed of fat and cut into bite-sized pieces

1 (10.5-ounce) can condensed French onion soup

1 (10.75-ounce) can condensed tomato soup

4 cups water

1½ (1-pound) bags frozen soup vegetables, thawed

¼ teaspoon freshly ground black pepper

2 tablespoons red wine or balsamic vinegar

1. Add the beef to the slow cooker along with the soups and water; stir to mix. Add the vegetables and pepper.

2. Cover and cook on low for 8 hours or until the beef is tender and the vegetables are cooked through. Stir in vinegar (as a flavor enhancer).

Quick and Easy Stew Too

1 (2-pound) chuck roast, trimmed of fat and cut into bite-sized pieces

1 (10.75-ounce) can condensed cream of celery soup

1 (10.75-ounce) can condensed cream of mushroom soup

1 (10.5-ounce) can condensed French onion soup

2 cups water

1½ (1-pound) bags frozen soup vegetables, thawed

¼ teaspoon freshly ground black pepper

1. Add the beef to the slow cooker along with the soups and water; stir to mix. Add the vegetables and pepper.

2. Cover and cook on low for 8 hours or until the beef is tender and the vegetables are cooked through.

Sour Cherry Beef Stew

¼ cup almond flour

½ teaspoon ground nutmeg

1 teaspoon ground cinnamon

½ teaspoon ground allspice

½ teaspoon ground black pepper

1 (2-pound) chuck steak, trimmed of fat and cut into 1" cubes

2 tablespoons olive oil

2 medium onions, peeled and chopped

2 (16-ounce) cans sour cherries (reserve half of the juice)

½ cup red wine

1 (14-ounce) can unsalted organic beef broth

2 pounds button mushrooms, cleaned and quartered

½ cup water

1. Combine almond flour, nutmeg, cinnamon, allspice, and pepper in a zip-top bag.
2. Add chuck steak to zip-top bag and shake to coat evenly.
3. Heat olive oil in a large skillet over medium-high heat.
4. Sear steak quickly in skillet for 1–2 minutes on each side. Remove from skillet and place in slow cooker.
5. Using the same skillet, cook onion on medium heat for 8 minutes.
6. Add cherries, juice, and red wine to the skillet and cook for 5 more minutes until the onions are browned.
7. Pour the cherry mixture into slow cooker.
8. Add broth, mushrooms, and water to slow cooker. Cook for at least 5 hours on low heat in slow cooker.

Slow Cooker Suggestions

Some chefs find it acceptable to use alcohol while cooking, since most of the alcohol is burned off. This is a nice way to bring some flavor to a dish without worrying about altering the recipe significantly.

CHAPTER 3

Casseroles, Ribs, and Chilis

Beef and Green Bean Casserole

SERVES 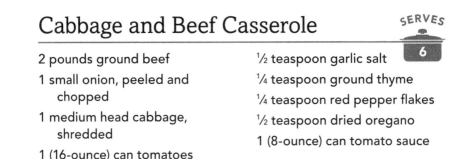 6

1 (1½-pound) round or sirloin steak, trimmed of fat and cut into short, thin strips

⅓ cup all-purpose flour

¼ teaspoon salt

¼ teaspoon freshly ground black pepper

1 medium green bell pepper, seeded and sliced

1 (15-ounce) can diced tomatoes

3 tablespoons soy sauce

1 large onion, peeled and sliced

8 ounces fresh mushrooms, cleaned and sliced

1 (10-ounce) package frozen French-style green beans, thawed

1. Add the steak strips, flour, salt, and pepper to the slow cooker; stir to coat the steak in the seasoned flour.

2. Add the bell pepper, tomatoes, soy sauce, onion, mushrooms, and green beans. Stir to combine. Cover and cook on low for 8 hours. Stir and taste for seasoning; add additional salt and pepper if needed.

Cabbage and Beef Casserole

SERVES 6

2 pounds ground beef

1 small onion, peeled and chopped

1 medium head cabbage, shredded

1 (16-ounce) can tomatoes

½ teaspoon garlic salt

¼ teaspoon ground thyme

¼ teaspoon red pepper flakes

½ teaspoon dried oregano

1 (8-ounce) can tomato sauce

1. In a large skillet over medium heat, brown the ground beef for about 5–6 minutes. Remove ground beef to a bowl and set aside. In same skillet sauté onion until softened, about 3–5 minutes.

2. In a greased 4–6-quart slow cooker, layer some of the onion, cabbage, tomatoes, garlic salt, thyme, red pepper flakes, oregano, and beef. Repeat layers, ending with beef. Pour tomato sauce over casserole.

3. Cook on low for 8 hours or on high for 4 hours.

Hamburger-Vegetable Casserole

Nonstick spray

2 large potatoes, scrubbed and sliced

3 large carrots, peeled and thinly sliced

1 cup frozen baby peas, thawed

1 large onion, peeled and diced

2 celery stalks, sliced

1 pound lean ground beef, browned and drained

1 (15.75-ounce) can cream of tomato soup or cream of mushroom soup

1 (15.75-ounce) can water

¼ teaspoon salt

¼ teaspoon freshly ground black pepper

1. Treat the slow cooker with nonstick spray. Add the potatoes, carrots, peas, onion, celery, and ground beef in layers in the order given.

2. In a medium bowl mix the soup with the water and then pour over the layers.

3. Cover and cook on low for 8 hours. Stir and taste for seasoning; add salt and pepper if needed.

Salisbury Steak Casserole

1 (10.5-ounce) can condensed French onion soup, divided

1½ pounds lean ground beef

½ cup bread crumbs

1 large egg

¼ teaspoon salt

¼ teaspoon freshly ground black pepper

Nonstick spray

1 (1-pound) bag frozen hash browns, thawed

1 (1-pound) bag frozen broccoli, green beans, onions, and peppers, thawed

¼ cup ketchup

¼ cup water

1 teaspoon Worcestershire sauce

½ teaspoon prepared mustard

1 tablespoon all-purpose flour

1 tablespoon butter, softened

2 tablespoons heavy cream

1. In a large bowl mix together half of the soup with the beef, bread crumbs, egg, salt, and pepper. Shape into 6 or 8 patties.

2. Add the patties to a nonstick skillet; brown on both sides over medium-high heat, and then pour off and discard any excess fat.

3. Treat the slow cooker with nonstick spray. Spread the hash browns over the bottom of the slow cooker. Top with the frozen vegetable mix. Arrange the browned meat patties over the vegetables.

4. In the soup can mix the remaining soup together with the ketchup, water, Worcestershire sauce, and mustard. Add the butter and flour to a small bowl; mix into a paste and then whisk in the heavy cream.

5. Add the flour mixture to the soup can and whisk to combine. Pour over the patties. Cover and cook on low for 8 hours.

Breakfast Casserole

1 pound 85% lean or higher ground beef

1 small onion, peeled and diced

1 teaspoon ground black pepper

1 teaspoon garlic powder

1 teaspoon red pepper flakes

12 large eggs

1 cup coconut milk

Canola oil for greasing the slow cooker (about 1 tablespoon)

1 small butternut squash, peeled, seeded, and sliced

1. In a large skillet over medium heat start to cook the ground beef. Add the onion and spices and cook just until the onion is soft, about 8–10 minutes (you don't need to finish cooking the beef—it will finish in the slow cooker).

2. In a large bowl whip together eggs and coconut milk.

3. Grease the inside of a 4–6-quart slow cooker. Put in the squash, the beef/onion mixture, and then the egg/milk mixture.

4. Stir and make sure that all of the food is covered by the egg/milk mixture. Cook on low for 8–10 hours. Slice and serve warm.

"French Fry" Casserole

1 pound ground beef

1 tablespoon coconut butter

½ medium onion, peeled and finely diced

1 cup sliced mushrooms

½ medium green pepper, seeded and diced

2 tablespoons arrowroot

1⅓ cups full-fat coconut milk

½ teaspoon ground black pepper

3 cups frozen sweet potato fries (shoestring cut)

1. Brown ground beef in a large skillet on medium heat for approximately 3–5 minutes. Pour cooked ground beef into a greased 2.5-quart or larger slow cooker.

2. In a medium saucepan over medium heat melt the coconut butter. Add the onion, mushrooms, and green pepper. Cook for 3–5 minutes until softened.

3. Mix the arrowroot with the coconut milk in a small bowl and slowly add to cooked vegetables. Whisk together for 5–10 minutes over medium heat until thickened.

4. Pour the cream sauce over ground beef in the slow cooker. Sprinkle with pepper.

5. Top casserole with sweet potato fries. Vent the lid of the slow cooker with a chopstick to prevent extra condensation on the fries. Cook on high for 3–4 hours or on low for 5–6 hours.

Lunch Casserole

1½ pounds lean ground beef

1 large onion, peeled and chopped

2 tablespoons canola oil

2 cloves garlic, peeled and minced

6 ounces sliced mushrooms

½ teaspoon ground nutmeg

1 (10-ounce) package frozen spinach, thawed and squeezed dry

3 tablespoons arrowroot

6 large eggs, beaten

¾ cup coconut milk, scalded

1. In a large skillet over medium heat lightly brown the beef and onions for 5–10 minutes in the canola oil.

2. Drain the excess fat and place meat mixture in a well-greased 2- or 4-quart slow cooker.

3. Stir the garlic, mushrooms, nutmeg, spinach, and arrowroot into the meat mixture in the slow cooker.

4. In a small bowl beat the eggs and coconut milk together. Pour over meat mixture in the slow cooker. Stir well.

5. Cover and cook on low for 7–9 hours or until firm.

Country Hamburger Casserole

4 large potatoes, peeled and sliced
3 large carrots, peeled and sliced
1 (16-ounce) can peas, drained
2 celery stalks, diced
2 medium onions, peeled and sliced
2 pounds ground beef, browned
1 (15-ounce) can evaporated milk
1 cup gluten-free chicken broth
3 tablespoons brown rice flour
½ teaspoon salt
½ teaspoon ground black pepper

1. Place potatoes in bottom of a greased 4-quart slow cooker; top with carrots, peas, celery, and onion slices. Place ground beef on top.
2. In a medium bowl whisk together milk, broth, flour, salt, and pepper and pour over ground beef.
3. Cover and cook on low for 6–8 hours. In the last 2 hours vent slow cooker lid with a chopstick to allow excess water to escape.

Slow Cooker Suggestions

Feel free to use ground turkey, ground pork, or ground sausage instead of ground beef. You can also make this a vegetarian casserole by using 2 cans of drained and rinsed navy beans instead of ground beef.

Pot-au-feu

2 tablespoons butter

1 (1-pound) bag baby carrots, divided

2 large onions, peeled and sliced, divided

4 celery stalks, finely diced

2 cloves garlic, peeled and chopped

1 bouquet garni

1 (2-pound) boneless chuck roast, trimmed of fat and
   cut into 1" pieces

8 chicken thighs

1 pound Western-style pork ribs

¼ teaspoon coarse sea salt

¼ teaspoon freshly ground black pepper

4 small turnips, peeled and quartered

1 medium rutabaga, peeled and cut into eighths

4 cups water

8 medium red or Yukon gold potatoes

1. Add the butter to a large (6.5-quart) slow cooker set on high. (You can make this dish in a 4-quart slow cooker, but you may need to omit the potatoes from the cooker and prepare them separately.) Finely dice 10 of the baby carrots and 2 of the onion slices.

2. Add the diced carrots, diced onion, and celery to the slow cooker; cover and cook for 15 minutes.

3. In this order, add the garlic, bouquet garni, beef, chicken, and pork; sprinkle the salt and pepper over the meat and then layer in the onion slices, remaining carrots, turnips, and rutabaga.

4. Pour in the water. (If you're using a 4-quart slow cooker, you can add the water in stages throughout the cooking process. Start with about 2 cups of the water and check the cooker every 2 hours to see if you need to add more to prevent it from boiling dry.)

continued on next page

5. Arrange the potatoes on top of the rutabaga. Reduce the heat setting to low, cover, and cook for 8 hours.

6. For a casual supper you can ladle servings directly from the crock. For a more formal dinner use a slotted spoon to arrange the vegetables and potatoes around the outside of a large serving platter with the meats arranged in the center; ladle a generous amount of the broth over all. Strain the remaining broth and pour the strained broth into a gravy boat to have at the table.

Slow Cooker Suggestions

Serve with toasted French bread rubbed with garlic and have coarse sea salt, cornichons, Dijon mustard, grated horseradish, pickled onions, sour cream, and whole-grain mustard at the table.

Taco Chili

SERVES 8

3 pounds lean ground beef

1 (1.2-ounce) package taco seasoning mix

2 (15-ounce) cans chunky Mexican-style tomatoes

1 (15-ounce) can red kidney beans

1 (15-ounce) can whole kernel corn

1. Brown the ground beef in a large nonstick skillet over medium heat, breaking apart the meat as you do so. Remove and discard any fat rendered from the meat before transferring it to the slow cooker.

2. Stir in the taco seasoning mix, tomatoes, kidney beans, and corn. Cover and cook on low for 4–6 hours.

Texas Firehouse Chili

SERVES 4

1 pound cubed lean beef

2 tablespoons onion powder

1 tablespoon garlic powder

2 tablespoons Mexican-style chili powder

1 tablespoon paprika

½ teaspoon dried oregano

½ teaspoon freshly ground black pepper

½ teaspoon ground white pepper

½ teaspoon ground cayenne pepper

½ teaspoon chipotle pepper

1 (8-ounce) can tomato sauce

1. Brown the beef in a large nonstick skillet over medium-high heat. Drain off any excess grease.

2. Add the meat and all of the remaining ingredients to a 4-quart slow cooker. Cook on low up to 10 hours.

Cincinnati Chili

1 pound 94% lean ground beef

1 (15-ounce) can crushed tomatoes in juice

2 cloves garlic, peeled and minced

1 medium onion, peeled and diced

1 teaspoon ground cumin

1 teaspoon cocoa powder

2 teaspoons chili powder

½ teaspoon ground cloves

1 tablespoon apple cider vinegar

1 teaspoon ground allspice

½ teaspoon ground cayenne pepper

1 teaspoon ground cinnamon

1 tablespoon Worcestershire sauce

¼ teaspoon salt

1. In a large nonstick skillet sauté the beef over medium heat until it is no longer pink. Drain all fat and discard it.
2. Place all ingredients—including the beef—in a 4-quart slow cooker. Stir. Cook on low for 8–10 hours.

Slow Cooker Suggestions

Even though it is not aesthetically necessary to brown the meat when making chili, sautéing meats before adding it to the slow cooker allows you to drain off any extra fat. Not only is it healthier to cook with less fat, but your chili will be unappetizingly greasy if there is too much fat present in the meat during cooking.

Secret Ingredient Beef Chili

1 pound 94% lean ground beef

2 (15-ounce) cans canned diced tomatoes

¼ cup cubed mango

1 teaspoon liquid smoke

1 teaspoon chili powder

1 teaspoon ground jalapeño powder

1 teaspoon hot chili powder

1 teaspoon smoked paprika

2 (15-ounce) cans kidney beans, drained and rinsed

1 medium onion, peeled and diced

3 cloves garlic, peeled and minced

1 teaspoon ground cumin

1. Sauté the beef in a large nonstick skillet over medium heat until no longer pink. Drain off all fat and discard it.
2. Place the beef and all the remaining ingredients in a 4-quart slow cooker. Stir. Cook on low for 8–10 hours.

Slow Cooker Suggestions

Canned beans are ready to eat directly out of the package, making them an excellent time-saver. Dried beans need to be soaked or cooked before using. Properly cooked dried beans can be substituted for an equal amount of canned, but resist the temptation to use uncooked dried beans unless explicitly directed to in the recipe. They may not rehydrate properly.

Lone Star State Chili

¼ pound bacon, diced

1 celery stalk, finely chopped

1 large carrot, peeled and finely chopped

1 (3-pound) chuck roast, trimmed of fat and cut into small cubes

2 large yellow onions, peeled and diced

6 cloves garlic, peeled and minced

6 small jalapeño peppers, seeded and diced

¼ teaspoon salt

¼ teaspoon freshly ground black pepper

4 tablespoons chili powder

1 teaspoon dried Mexican oregano

1 teaspoon ground cumin

1 teaspoon brown sugar

1 (28-ounce) can diced tomatoes

1 cup beef broth

1. Add all of the ingredients to the slow cooker in the order given and stir to combine. The liquid in your slow cooker should completely cover the meat and vegetables.

2. If additional liquid is needed, add more crushed tomatoes, broth, or some water. Cover and cook on low for 8 hours.

3. Taste for seasoning and add more chili powder if desired.

Slow Cooker Suggestions

Wear gloves or sandwich bags over your hands when you clean and dice hot peppers. It's important to avoid having the peppers come into contact with any of your skin, or especially your eyes. As an added precaution, wash your hands (and under your fingernails) thoroughly with hot soapy water after you remove the gloves or sandwich bags.

Enchilada Chili

1 (2-pound) boneless chuck roast, cut into bite-sized pieces

1 (15-ounce) can pinto and/or red kidney beans, drained and rinsed

1 (15-ounce) can diced tomatoes, undrained

1 (10.5-ounce) can condensed beef broth

1 (10-ounce) can enchilada sauce

1 large onion, peeled and chopped

2 cloves garlic, peeled and minced

1 cup water

4 tablespoons fine cornmeal or masa harina (corn flour)

2 tablespoons minced fresh cilantro

1 cup grated queso blanco or Monterey jack cheese

1. Add the beef, beans, tomatoes, broth, enchilada sauce, onion, garlic, and water to the slow cooker. Cover and cook on low for 8 hours.

2. In a small bowl whisk the cornmeal together with enough cold water to make a paste; stir some of the liquid from the slow cooker into the cornmeal paste and then whisk it into the chili.

3. Cook and stir on high for 15–30 minutes or until chili is thickened and the raw cornmeal taste is cooked out of the chili.

4. Top each serving with minced cilantro and grated cheese.

Hearty Beef Chili

1 pound ground beef

1 cup chopped onion

¾ cup chopped green pepper

1 clove garlic, peeled and minced

1 (16-ounce) can diced tomatoes

1 (16-ounce) can pinto beans

1 (8-ounce) can tomato sauce

2 teaspoons chili powder

½ teaspoon dried basil

1. Brown ground beef and onion in a large skillet over medium heat, approximately 5–6 minutes. Leave the ground beef in larger chunks when cooking instead of breaking it down into very small pieces. Add cooked beef and onion to a greased 4-quart slow cooker.

2. Add remaining ingredients. Cover and cook on high for 4 hours or on low for 8 hours.

Slow Cooker Suggestions

Some people prefer to use all beef in their chili. For a full-beef, bean-free chili, use 2 pounds of ground beef and leave out the pinto beans. Quartered button mushrooms can also add a meaty texture to this chili.

Dueling Flavors Chili

1 pound ground chuck

1 pound ground pork

2 large yellow onions, peeled and diced

6 cloves garlic, peeled and minced

1 teaspoon whole cumin seeds

2 tablespoons chili powder

¼ teaspoon dried oregano

1 (28-ounce) can diced tomatoes

¼ cup ketchup

¼ teaspoon ground cinnamon

¼ teaspoon ground cloves

2 tablespoons brown sugar

2 (15-ounce) cans kidney beans, drained and rinsed

1 (14-ounce) can lower-sodium beef broth

1 tablespoon Worcestershire sauce

Water as needed

Dash hot sauce

¼ teaspoon salt

¼ teaspoon freshly ground black pepper

1. Add the ground chuck, pork, onions, garlic, cumin seeds, chili powder, and oregano to a large nonstick skillet; cook over medium heat until the beef and pork are browned and cooked through. Drain off any excess fat and discard. Transfer to the slow cooker.

2. Stir in the tomatoes, ketchup, cinnamon, cloves, brown sugar, kidney beans, beef broth, and Worcestershire sauce.

3. Add enough water as needed to bring the liquid level to the top of the beans and meat. Cover and cook on low for 8 hours.

4. Taste for seasoning and add hot sauce and salt and pepper if needed. You may also wish to add more brown sugar or chili powder according to your taste.

Chili con Carne

2 tablespoons peanut oil

1 pound lean ground beef

1 large yellow onion, peeled and chopped

3 tablespoons chili powder

1 teaspoon ground cumin

3 cloves garlic, peeled and diced

1 tablespoon Worcestershire sauce

1 (28-ounce) can chopped tomatoes

1 large green pepper, seeded and chopped

1 (15-ounce) can kidney beans, drained and rinsed

¼ teaspoon salt

¼ teaspoon freshly ground black pepper

1 teaspoon granulated or light brown sugar

1. Add the oil to a Dutch oven over medium heat.
2. Add the ground beef, onion, chili power, and cumin.
3. When the meat is cooked and the onions are transparent, drain any excess fat from the pan. Add the remaining ingredients and stir to combine.
4. Place in slow cooker, cover, and cook at low setting 1–2 hours, stirring occasionally. Taste and adjust seasoning if necessary before serving.

CHAPTER 4

Meatloaf and Meatball Recipes

61

Barbecue Meatloaf

2 pounds lean ground beef

½ pound lean ground pork

2 large eggs

1 large yellow onion, peeled and diced

¼ teaspoon salt

¼ teaspoon freshly ground black pepper

1½ cups quick-cooking oatmeal

1 teaspoon dried parsley

1½ cups barbecue sauce, divided

1 tablespoon brown sugar

¼ teaspoon Mrs. Dash Extra Spicy Seasoning Blend

1. Add the ground beef, ground pork, eggs, onion, salt, pepper, oatmeal, parsley, and 1 cup of the barbecue sauce to a large bowl; mix well with your hands. Form into a loaf to fit the size (round or oval) of your slow cooker.

2. Line the slow cooker with two pieces of heavy-duty aluminum foil long enough to reach up the sides of the slow cooker and over the edge, crossing one piece over the other. Place a piece of nonstick foil the size of the bottom of the slow cooker crock inside the crossed pieces of foil or a slow cooker liner to form a platform for the meatloaf. (This is to make it easier to lift the meatloaf out of the slow cooker.)

3. Put the meatloaf on top of the nonstick foil. Spread the remaining ½ cup barbecue sauce over the top of the meatloaf.

4. Sprinkle the brown sugar and Mrs. Dash Extra Spicy Seasoning Blend on top of the barbecue sauce. Cover and cook on low for 8 hours or until the internal temperature of the meatloaf registers 165°F.

5. Lift the meatloaf out of the slow cooker and place it on a cooling rack. Allow it to rest for 20 minutes before transferring it to a serving platter and slicing it.

Zesty Meatloaf

2 pounds lean ground beef

1 large egg

1 (10.5-ounce) can condensed French onion soup

¼ teaspoon salt

¼ teaspoon freshly ground black pepper

2 cups herb-seasoned stuffing mix or crushed seasoned croutons

1 (15-ounce) can tomato sauce

2 tablespoons Worcestershire sauce

⅓ cup brown sugar

2 tablespoons red wine or balsamic vinegar

¼ teaspoon Mrs. Dash Extra Spicy Seasoning Blend

1. Add the beef, egg, onion soup, salt, pepper, and stuffing mix or crushed croutons to a large bowl; mix well with your hands. Form into a loaf to fit the size (round or oval) of your slow cooker.

2. Put the meatloaf in the slow cooker. Add the tomato sauce, Worcestershire sauce, brown sugar, vinegar, and Mrs. Dash Extra Spicy Seasoning Blend to a bowl and stir to mix. Pour over the meatloaf.

3. Cover and cook on low for 7 hours or until the internal temperature of the meatloaf registers 165°F. Slice and serve with the sauce from the slow cooker.

Country Meatloaf

1 pound lean ground beef

½ pound lean ground pork

¾ teaspoon salt

¼ teaspoon ground black pepper

1 medium yellow onion, peeled and finely chopped

1 celery stalk, very finely chopped

½ cup grated carrot

1 small green pepper, seeded and finely chopped

1 large egg

½ cup plus ⅓ cup ketchup, divided

½ cup tomato sauce

½ cup quick-cooking oatmeal

½ cup crumbled butter-flavor crackers

Nonstick spray

2 tablespoons brown sugar

1 tablespoon prepared mustard

1. Add the ground beef and pork, salt, black pepper, onion, celery, carrot, green pepper, egg, ½ cup ketchup, tomato sauce, oatmeal, and cracker crumbs into a large bowl and mix well.

2. Treat the slow cooker with nonstick spray. Add the meat mixture and shape the meatloaf to fit the crock of the slow cooker.

3. In a small bowl mix together the ⅓ cup ketchup, brown sugar, and mustard; spread it over the top of the meatloaf. Cover and cook on low for 7 hours or until the meat is cooked through. Use paper towels to blot and remove any fat that's rendered from the meat. Let the meatloaf sit for 30 minutes and then slice and serve.

Slow Cooker Suggestions

There will be room on top of the Country Meatloaf to add 3 large, peeled, and sliced carrots and 6 medium peeled potatoes. You may need to increase the cooking time to 8 hours if you add the vegetables.

Meatloaf-Stuffed Green Peppers

SERVES 4

¼ cup almond flour

¼ cup coconut milk

1 pound ground beef

½ teaspoon lemon juice

½ teaspoon ground black pepper

1½ teaspoons dried onion

1 large egg

4 medium green peppers

⅓ cup water

1. In a large bowl mix together the almond flour and coconut milk; set aside for 5 minutes.
2. Add the ground beef, lemon juice, black pepper, dried onion, and egg to the mixture. Mix together well.
3. Carefully remove the tops, seeds, and membranes of the peppers. Fill each pepper with equal amounts of the meatloaf mixture.
4. Place the stuffed peppers in a greased 4-quart slow cooker. Add ⅓ cup water around the bottom of the stuffed peppers.
5. Cook on high for 3–4 hours or on low for 6–8 hours until green peppers are softened and the meat is cooked through.

Italian Meatloaf

Nonstick cooking spray

1 large onion, peeled and cut into rings

2 pounds 94% lean ground beef

1 large egg

¼ cup bread crumbs

1 tablespoon dried Italian seasoning

1 teaspoon dried oregano

1 teaspoon red pepper flakes

1 teaspoon ground fennel seed

1 teaspoon dried rosemary

¼ teaspoon freshly ground black pepper

⅛ teaspoon salt

½ cup diced onion

1 clove garlic, peeled and minced

¼ cup dry-packed sun-dried tomatoes, diced

3 ounces tomato paste

1 tablespoon Worcestershire sauce

1. Spray a 6-quart oval slow cooker with cooking spray. Line the bottom of the cooker with the onion rings.

2. In a large bowl mix the ground beef, egg, bread crumbs, Italian seasoning, oregano, red pepper flakes, fennel seed, rosemary, black pepper, salt, diced onion, garlic, and sun-dried tomatoes until well combined. Mold into a loaf shape and place on top of the sliced onions.

3. In a small bowl whisk the tomato paste and Worcestershire sauce. Brush over the top and visible sides of the meatloaf.

4. Cook for 4–6 hours on low or until the meat is thoroughly cooked. Remove the meatloaf from the slow cooker and slice. Discard the onion rings and any juices on the bottom of the pan.

Slow Cooker Suggestions

To change this to a Southwestern variation, substitute ⅓ cup black beans for the sun-dried tomatoes. Also substitute 1 teaspoon each of ground chipotle pepper, hot paprika, and ground jalapeño for the oregano, Italian seasoning, rosemary, and fennel. For the topping, whisk the tomato paste with 1 teaspoon hot sauce and 1 teaspoon water.

Light and Creamy Swedish Meatballs

SERVES
20

2 thin slices white sandwich bread

½ cup 1% milk

2 pounds 94% lean ground beef or ground chicken

2 cloves garlic, peeled and minced

1 large egg

½ teaspoon ground allspice, divided

¼ teaspoon ground nutmeg, divided

3 cups chicken stock

1 (12-ounce) can fat-free evaporated milk

1 tablespoon butter, melted

⅓ cup all-purpose flour

1. Preheat oven to 350°F. In a shallow saucepan cook the bread and milk on low until the milk is absorbed, about 1 minute. Place the bread into a large bowl and add the meat, garlic, egg, ¼ teaspoon allspice, and ⅛ teaspoon nutmeg.

2. Mix until all ingredients are evenly distributed. Roll into 1" balls. Line two baking sheets with parchment paper.

3. Place the meatballs in a single layer on the baking sheets. Bake for 15 minutes and then drain on paper towel–lined plates.

4. Meanwhile, bring the stock, evaporated milk, butter, and remaining nutmeg and allspice to a simmer in a small saucepan. Whisk in the flour and continue to whisk until the mixture is slightly thickened. Remove from heat.

5. Place the meatballs into a 4- or 6-quart oval slow cooker. Pour the sauce over the meatballs. Cook on low up to 6 hours. Stir gently before serving to distribute the sauce evenly.

Appetizer Meatballs

YIELDS

24

MEATBALLS

1 pound lean ground beef
1 large egg
2 tablespoons dried minced onion
1 teaspoon garlic powder
1/2 teaspoon ground black pepper

1. Add all the ingredients to a large mixing bowl and combine with your clean hands. Shape the resulting mixture into approximately 24 meatballs.
2. Add meatballs to a 2- to 4-quart slow cooker, cover, and cook on high until meatballs are cooked through, about 4 hours.
3. Turn heat to low and keep warm before serving.

Barbecue Meatballs

SERVES

4

1½ cups chili sauce
1 cup fig jam or grape jelly
2 teaspoons Dijon mustard
1 pound lean ground beef

1 large egg
3 tablespoons arrowroot
1/2 teaspoon lemon juice

1. Preheat oven to 400°F.
2. Combine the chili sauce, jam, and mustard in a 2-quart slow cooker and stir well.
3. Cover and cook on high while preparing meatballs.
4. In a large mixing bowl combine the remaining ingredients thoroughly. Shape into 20 medium-sized meatballs. Place meatballs on a broiler rack or in a baking pan and bake in the oven for 15–20 minutes. Drain well.
5. Add meatballs to the sauce in slow cooker. Stir well to coat.
6. Cover and cook on low for 6–10 hours.

Slow-Cooked Meatballs

1½ pounds lean ground beef

1 cup uncooked long-grain white rice

1 small yellow onion, peeled and finely chopped

3 cloves garlic, peeled and minced

2 teaspoons dried parsley

½ tablespoon dried dill

1 large egg

¼ cup all-purpose flour

2 cups tomato juice or tomato-vegetable juice

2–4 cups water

2 tablespoons butter

¼ teaspoon each salt and freshly ground black pepper

1. Make the meatballs by mixing the ground beef with the rice, onion, garlic, parsley, dill, and egg; shape into small meatballs and roll each one in flour.

2. Add the tomato or tomato-vegetable juice to a 4-quart slow cooker. Carefully add the meatballs. Pour in enough water to completely cover the meatballs. Add the butter.

3. Cover and cook on low for 6–8 hours, checking periodically to make sure the cooker doesn't boil dry. Taste for seasoning and add salt and pepper if needed.

Pineapple Sausage Meatballs

1 (20-ounce) can crushed pineapple packed in juice, drained

¼ cup dried minced onion

1 cup ketchup

2 cups barbecue sauce, divided

1 tablespoon brown sugar

1 teaspoon chili powder

¼ teaspoon Mrs. Dash Extra Spicy Seasoning Blend

1 pound lean ground beef

1 pound lean ground pork

2 large eggs

1 large yellow onion, peeled and diced

¼ teaspoon each salt and freshly ground black pepper

1½ cups quick-cooking oatmeal

1 teaspoon dried parsley

1. Add the drained crushed pineapple, dried onion, ketchup, 1 cup of the barbecue sauce, brown sugar, chili powder, and Mrs. Dash Extra Spicy Seasoning Blend to the slow cooker. Cover and cook on low while you make the meatballs.

2. Preheat the oven to 425°F. Add the remaining 1 cup barbecue sauce, ground beef, ground pork, eggs, diced onion, salt, pepper, oatmeal, and parsley to a large bowl; use hands to mix.

3. Form into 24 meatballs. Place on a baking sheet; bake for 10 minutes or until browned on the outside but still rare on the inside.

4. Add the browned meatballs to the sauce. Cover and cook on low for 3 hours.

Retro Meatballs

2 tablespoons extra-virgin olive oil or vegetable oil

2 pounds frozen precooked meatballs

1 (12-ounce) jar chili sauce

1 cup grape jelly

1. Add the oil to the bag of frozen meatballs; close and toss to coat the meatballs in the oil. Add to the slow cooker.
2. Cover and cook on high for 4 hours. Carefully stir the meatballs every hour to rearrange them in the cooker.
3. In a measuring cup or bowl mix the chili sauce together with the grape jelly. Pour over the meatballs in the slow cooker.
4. Cover and cook on low for 2 hours or until the sauce is heated through and thickened. To serve, reduce the heat setting of the slow cooker to warm.

Slow Cooker Suggestions

For In a Hurry Retro Meatballs, preheat the oven to 425°F. Arrange the oil-coated frozen meatballs on a baking sheet; bake for 30 minutes, use tongs to turn the meatballs, and continue to bake for 15–30 minutes or until warmed through. Add the meatballs to the slow cooker and continue with Step 2 of the Retro Meatballs recipe.

Meatball Sandwiches

1 (38-ounce) bag frozen precooked meatballs

1 (48-ounce) jar pasta sauce

French bread or garlic toast

2 tablespoons freshly grated Parmigiano-Reggiano cheese

1. Put the frozen meatballs in the slow cooker. Pour the pasta sauce over the meatballs. Cover and cook on low for 8 hours or until the meatballs are thawed and heated through.
2. Serve the meatballs and sauce between 2 slices of French bread or garlic toast. Sprinkle Parmigiano-Reggiano cheese over the meatballs.

Meatballs in Chipotle Sauce

1 tablespoon vegetable oil

1 large onion, peeled and thinly sliced

3 teaspoons garlic powder, divided

2 tablespoons chili powder, divided

¼ teaspoon dried Mexican oregano

2 chipotle peppers in adobo sauce

1 (28-ounce) can crushed tomatoes

1 cup chicken broth

¼ teaspoon each salt and freshly ground black pepper

1½ pounds lean ground beef

½ pound ground pork

1 large egg

1 small white onion, peeled and diced

10 soda crackers, crumbled

1. Add the vegetable oil and sliced onions to the slow cooker; stir to coat the onions in the oil. Cover and cook on high for 30 minutes or until the onions are transparent. Stir in 1½ teaspoons garlic powder, 1 tablespoon chili powder, and oregano. Cover and cook on high for 15 minutes.

2. Stir in the chipotles in adobo sauce, tomatoes, broth, salt, and pepper. Cover and cook on high while you prepare the meatballs.

3. Preheat oven to 425°F. Add the ground beef, ground pork, egg, diced onion, 1 tablespoon chili powder, 1½ teaspoons garlic powder, and crumbled crackers to a large bowl; use hands to mix.

4. Form into 18 meatballs. Place on a baking sheet; bake for 10 minutes or until browned on the outside but still rare on the inside.

5. Use an immersion blender to purée the sauce in the slow cooker. Add the browned meatballs to the sauce. Cover and cook on low for 3 hours.

Slow Cooker Suggestions

You can add extra heat to the sauce by adding more than 2 of the canned chipotles or some Mrs. Dash Extra Spicy Seasoning Blend.

Paleo Meatballs and Sauce

1 (16-ounce) can diced, no-salt-added tomatoes

1 (4-ounce) can organic, no-salt-added tomato paste

2 pounds grass-fed ground beef

1 cup chopped celery

1 cup chopped onion

1 cup chopped carrots

4 cloves garlic, peeled and finely chopped

3 large eggs

½ cup flaxseed meal

1 tablespoon dried oregano

1 teaspoon ground black pepper

¼ teaspoon chili powder

1. Pour canned tomatoes and tomato paste into a 4-quart slow cooker.
2. Place all remaining ingredients in a large bowl and mix well with clean hands.
3. Roll resulting meat mixture into 2–3-ounce (large, rounded tablespoon) balls and add to slow cooker.
4. Cook on low for 5 hours minimum.

Tipsy Meatballs

SERVES
8–10

2 large onions, peeled and chopped

1 (16-ounce) package frozen meatballs

1 (12-ounce) can beer

1 cup ketchup

½ cup chili sauce

2 tablespoons prepared mustard

¼ cup pickle relish

1. Place onions in 4-quart slow cooker. Add meatballs. In a medium bowl combine remaining ingredients and pour into slow cooker.

2. Cover and cook on low for 5–7 hours until meatballs are hot and tender. Serve with toothpicks.

Regal Caper Sauce

YIELDS
3 C

3 tablespoons butter, divided

2 tablespoons flour

3 cups beef stock, divided

½ teaspoon salt

½ teaspoon black peppercorns

1 large egg yolk

6 tablespoons capers

1. Melt 2 tablespoons butter in a saucepan over medium heat and mix in the flour, stirring until the flour is well mixed and slightly browned. Add 1 cup of the stock and mix well, then transfer to the slow cooker.

2. Add salt, peppercorns, and remaining 2 cups stock. Cover and heat on low for 1–2 hours.

3. Half an hour before serving, skim with a strainer. Stir in the yolk and 1 tablespoon butter, then add the capers.

Gedilla's Meatballs in Borscht

1 large onion, peeled and finely chopped (about 1 cup), divided

2 large carrots, peeled and chopped

2 large beets, peeled and shredded

2 cups shredded cabbage

1 tablespoon olive oil

2 tablespoons sugar

1 teaspoon kosher salt

2 tablespoons fresh lemon juice

1 bay leaf

1 pound ground beef

1 egg, lightly beaten

½ cup matzo meal

¼ teaspoon ground black pepper

½ cup tomato juice

4 cups beef broth or water

2 cups matzo farfel (for garnish)

1. Add ¾ cup of the chopped onion, the carrots, the beets, and the cabbage to a 4-quart slow cooker. Drizzle in the olive oil; stir to combine. Sprinkle on the sugar, salt, and lemon juice; add the bay leaf. Set aside.

2. In a large bowl combine the ground beef, egg, remaining onion, matzo meal, and pepper. Using your hands, roll the mixture into balls about 1" in diameter. Place meatballs on top of the vegetables in the slow cooker.

3. Pour the tomato juice and the broth or water over the meatballs. Cover and cook on low for 6–8 hours or on high for 3–4 hours or until the meatballs are fully cooked and the vegetables are tender.

4. Serve meatballs with some of the broth and vegetables. Sprinkle on the matzo farfel just before serving.

Meatballs with Mushrooms

1 pound ground beef

1 clove garlic, peeled and minced

¼ cup chopped celery

½ cup uncooked rice

½ cup bread crumbs

½ teaspoon ground sage

½ teaspoon ground white pepper

½ teaspoon salt

4 tablespoons vegetable oil, divided

½ pound mushrooms, cleaned and minced

1 medium onion, peeled and minced

1 tablespoon flour

1 cup water

1 cup tomato sauce

1. Combine the meat, garlic, celery, rice, bread crumbs, spices, and salt in a large bowl; mix together with your hands.
2. Form into ¾" balls. Brown in 2 tablespoons vegetable oil in a large pan over medium heat and drain. Arrange in the slow cooker.
3. Sauté the mushrooms and onion in 2 tablespoons vegetable oil in a large pan over medium heat. Add the flour to the mushroom mixture and stir to thicken. Add the water and tomato sauce to this slowly and mix until smooth.
4. Pour the tomato and mushroom mixture over meatballs.
5. Cover and heat on low for 3–4 hours.

Slow Cooker Suggestions

Rice is nice, especially when it's made in a slow cooker. Use converted rice (not instant) and it will come out light and fluffy. You can also add vegetables and spices to the rice for an easy meal.

Royal Meatballs

1 medium onion, peeled and minced

6 medium shallots, peeled and minced

3 tablespoons butter

$\frac{1}{2}$ pound ground lamb

$\frac{1}{2}$ pound ground veal

$\frac{1}{2}$ pound bacon, minced

1 small bunch parsley, finely chopped

12 anchovies, finely chopped

$\frac{1}{4}$ cup finely chopped chives

1 clove garlic, peeled and minced

$\frac{1}{2}$ teaspoon salt

$\frac{1}{4}$ teaspoon ground black pepper

$\frac{1}{4}$ teaspoon ground nutmeg

$\frac{1}{8}$ teaspoon ground cayenne pepper

$\frac{1}{2}$ cup water

2 large eggs

3 cups Regal Caper Sauce (see recipe in this chapter)

1. Sauté the onion and shallots in the butter in a medium pan over medium heat until soft. Transfer the onion and shallots to a mixing bowl and set aside the pan with remaining butter.

2. Combine all ingredients except Regal Caper Sauce with the onion mixture in the mixing bowl and mix well. Form into $\frac{3}{4}$" balls. Heat the meatballs in the pan over medium heat until browned, then drain excess grease.

3. Arrange the meatballs in the slow cooker and cover with Regal Caper Sauce.

4. Cover and heat on low for 3–4 hours.

Paprika Meatballs

SERVES
8

1 pound ground veal

1 pound ground pork

1 clove garlic, peeled and minced

¼ pound grated mozzarella cheese

3 large eggs

1 tablespoon paprika

1 teaspoon salt

1 cup bread crumbs

½ cup milk

2 tablespoons vegetable oil

2 medium tomatoes, diced

1 cup tomato sauce

1. Combine the meat, garlic, and cheese in a mixing bowl with the eggs, paprika, salt, bread crumbs, and milk; mix well.
2. Form into ¾" balls and sauté in oil in a large pan over medium heat until browned. Drain grease, then arrange the meatballs in the slow cooker.
3. Pour the tomatoes and tomato sauce over the meatballs.
4. Cover and heat on low for 3–4 hours.

Slow Cooker Suggestions

Pasta is a great addition to slow-cooked meals, but it should not be made in your slow cooker. To serve pasta with a dish, cook the pasta separately, then serve on the side, or add it to the slow cooker just before serving. If the pasta is coated with a little butter or oil, it can be kept warm by itself in a slow cooker.

78 Slow Cooker Favorites: Beef

Sweet Buttermilk Meatballs

1 medium onion, peeled and minced

2 pounds ground beef

1 cup bread crumbs

½ cup milk

1 teaspoon plus ¼ teaspoon salt, divided

¼ teaspoon plus ⅛ teaspoon ground black pepper, divided

3 tablespoons plus ¼ cup butter, divided

¼ cup flour

2¼ cups buttermilk

2 tablespoons sugar

1½ teaspoons dry mustard

1 large egg

1. Mix the onion, ground beef, bread crumbs, milk, 1 teaspoon salt, and ¼ teaspoon black pepper in a large bowl. Form into ¾" balls.

2. Sauté the meatballs in 3 tablespoons butter in a pan over medium heat until browned; drain and discard the grease. Transfer the meatballs to the slow cooker.

3. Add the remaining ¼ cup butter to the pan and melt it over low heat. Stir in the flour until well blended.

4. Slowly add the buttermilk to the flour mixture; blend well. Add the sugar, ¼ teaspoon salt, ⅛ teaspoon pepper, mustard, and egg; stir over low heat to thicken. Pour the sauce over the meatballs in the slow cooker.

5. Cover and heat on low for 2–3 hours.

Slow Cooker Suggestions

Plan for steam. Once all of those slow cookers are opened up, the steamy aromas may warm up your party rooms. Be sure you have enough ventilation or air conditioning to keep the temperature and humidity comfortable for your guests.

Sherry Meatballs

6 slices bacon

2 medium onions, peeled and diced

2 cloves garlic, peeled and diced

1 cup bread crumbs

2 pounds ground beef

2 large eggs

1 teaspoon salt

½ teaspoon ground black pepper

½ teaspoon dried oregano

1 pound mushrooms, cleaned and sliced

3 tablespoons butter

2 tablespoons flour

½ cup milk

½ cup water

½ cup sherry

1. Heat the bacon in a pan over medium heat until browned. Remove the browned slices from the pan to drain; set aside most of the bacon fat to use later.

2. Sauté the onion and garlic in the remaining bacon fat; then remove the onion mixture from the pan and add it with the bread crumbs, beef, eggs, salt, pepper, and oregano into a mixing bowl.

3. Form the meat mixture into ¾" balls. Sauté the balls in the bacon fat you set aside over medium heat; drain. Crumble the bacon; arrange the meatballs in the slow cooker with the crumbled bacon.

4. Sauté the mushrooms in butter in a medium pan over medium heat until browned; stir in the flour and allow the juices to thicken. Slowly stir in the milk and water. Pour the thickened mushroom sauce over the meatballs in the slow cooker.

5. Cover and heat on low for 2–3 hours.

6. Half an hour before serving add the sherry.

CHAPTER 5

Roasts and Ragouts

Apple-Mustard Beef Brisket

SERVES

8

1 (3-pound) beef brisket

1 large yellow onion, peeled and quartered

2 large cloves garlic, peeled and minced

4 large cloves garlic, peeled and left whole

1 (10-ounce) jar apple jelly

3 tablespoons Dijon mustard

¼ teaspoon each salt and freshly ground black pepper

¾ teaspoon curry powder

⅓ cup dry white wine

1 cup apple juice

1 cup water

2 apples, peeled, cored, and sliced

1. Add all ingredients to the slow cooker in the order given, layering the apple slices on top of the meat.

2. Cover and cook on low for 8 hours or until meat is tender.

Slow Cooker Suggestions

Brisket will become even more moist and tender if you allow it to cool in the broth, so this makes a good dish to make the day before. To reheat it, bake it for 45 minutes at 325°F. Baste it with some additional sauce and put it under the broiler for a few minutes to allow the meat to develop a glaze.

Beef Brisket with Beer

SERVES

6

1 (3-pound) beef brisket, cut into serving-sized pieces

½ teaspoon seasoning salt

¾ cup brown sugar

1 medium onion, peeled and thinly sliced

1 (12-ounce) can beer

1. Rub the beef with seasoning salt and brown sugar. Arrange the beef and onion in the slow cooker and add the beer.

2. Cover and cook on low for 6–8 hours.

Herbed Pot Roast

2 celery stalks, diced

1 (3-pound) boneless chuck roast

¼ teaspoon each salt and freshly ground black pepper

2 large yellow onions, peeled and quartered

2 cloves garlic, peeled and minced

2 cups beef broth

¼ cup red wine vinegar

1 teaspoon dried thyme

8 medium red potatoes

2 pounds baby carrots

¼ cup butter, softened

¼ cup all-purpose flour

1. Add the celery, roast, salt, pepper, onion, garlic, broth, vinegar, and thyme to a 4-quart slow cooker. Cover and cook on low for 6 hours.

2. Wash the potatoes and peel off a strip of the skin from around each one. Add potatoes to the slow cooker along with the baby carrots. Cover and cook for an additional 2 hours on low.

3. If you wish to thicken the pan juices to make gravy, use a slotted spoon to transfer the meat and vegetables to a serving platter; keep warm.

4. Strain the pan juices and return 1½ cups to the slow cooker. Increase the temperature on the slow cooker to high and bring to a boil.

5. In a small bowl use a fork to blend together the butter and flour. Whisk the flour mixture into the boiling juices 1 teaspoon at a time. Once you've added all of the mixture, boil for 1 minute and then reduce the setting to low. Stir and simmer for 2–3 more minutes or until the mixture is thickened. Taste for seasoning and add salt and pepper if desired.

Slow Cooker Suggestions

To turn this recipe into an Iranian Beef Roast, in Step 1 omit the thyme and add a small can of diced tomatoes, ⅓ cup fresh snipped cilantro, ¾ teaspoon freshly ground black pepper, ¾ teaspoon ground cumin, ½ teaspoon ground coriander, ¼ teaspoon ground cloves, and a pinch each of ground cardamom, ground nutmeg, and ground cinnamon. In Step 2 substitute thawed frozen green beans for the carrots.

Onion Pot Roast

1 (1-pound) bag baby carrots

2 celery stalks, diced

1 medium green bell pepper, seeded and diced

1 large yellow onion, peeled and sliced

1 (3-pound) boneless chuck roast, trimmed of fat and cut into serving-sized portions

1 envelope onion soup mix

$\frac{1}{2}$ teaspoon ground black pepper

1 cup water

1 cup tomato juice

2 cloves garlic, peeled and minced

1 tablespoon Worcestershire sauce

1 tablespoon steak sauce

1. Add the carrots, celery, green bell pepper, and onion to the slow cooker. Place the roast pieces on top of the vegetables and sprinkle with soup mix and black pepper.

2. Add the water, tomato juice, garlic, Worcestershire sauce, and steak sauce to a bowl or measuring cup; mix well and then pour into the slow cooker. Cover and cook on low for 8 hours.

Slow Cooker Suggestions

Reheat leftover pan juices from the Onion Pot Roast and serve it as a sauce in which to dip roast beef sandwiches. Be sure to have horseradish and mayonnaise available for those who want to add it to their sandwiches.

Pot Roast in Fruit-Infused Gravy

2 cloves garlic, peeled and minced

1 teaspoon ground sage

½ teaspoon salt

½ teaspoon freshly ground black pepper

⅛ teaspoon ground cayenne pepper

1 (3-pound) boneless chuck roast

2 tablespoons vegetable oil

1 cup beef broth

1 large onion, peeled and diced

1 cup halved pitted prunes (dried plums)

2 large apples, peeled, cored, and cut into thick slices

1 pound parsnips, peeled and cut into ½" pieces

1 (1-pound) bag baby carrots

¼ cup butter

¼ cup all-purpose flour

1 tablespoon balsamic vinegar

1. In a small bowl stir together garlic, sage, salt, black pepper, and cayenne. Spread the garlic mixture over both sides of the meat. Add the oil to a large skillet and bring it to temperature over medium-high heat; add the roast and brown it on both sides. Add the browned roast to the slow cooker.

2. Pour the broth over roast. Add the onion, prunes, apples, parsnips, and baby carrots. Cover and cook on low for 8 hours.

3. With a slotted spoon transfer the meat and vegetables to a serving platter; cover and keep warm.

4. Skim the fat off the juices that remain in the pan. Add water if necessary to bring the pan juices to 1½ cups. Increase the heat setting to high; cover and cook until the liquid bubbles around the edges.

5. In a bowl mix the butter, flour, and ½ cup of the pan juices together and then whisk into the slow cooker. Cook, stirring constantly, for 15 minutes or until the flour taste is cooked out of the gravy and it's thickened enough to coat the back of a spoon. Taste for seasoning and add salt and pepper if necessary.

6. Stir in the balsamic vinegar. Serve the gravy over the roast, vegetables, and fruit.

Yankee Pot Roast

¼ pound salt pork or bacon, cut into cubes

2 celery stalks, diced

1 (4-pound) chuck or English roast

¼ teaspoon each salt and freshly ground black pepper

2 large onions, peeled and quartered

1 (1-pound) bag baby carrots

2 turnips, peeled and diced

8 medium potatoes, peeled

2 cups beef broth

4 tablespoons butter

4 tablespoons all-purpose flour

1. Add the salt pork or bacon and the celery to the bottom of the slow cooker. Place the roast on top of the pork; sprinkle with salt and pepper. Add the onion, carrots, turnips, and potatoes. Pour in the beef broth. Cover and cook on low for 8 hours.

2. Use a slotted spoon to move the meat and vegetables to a serving platter; cover and keep warm.

3. In a small bowl mix the butter and flour together with ½ cup of the broth. Increase the slow cooker heat setting to high; cover and cook until the mixture begins to bubble around the edges.

4. Whisk the flour mixture into the broth; cook, stirring constantly, for 10 minutes or until the flour flavor is cooked out of the gravy and it's thickened enough to coat the back of a spoon. Taste the gravy for seasoning and stir in more salt and pepper if needed. Serve over or alongside the meat and vegetables.

Slow Cooker Suggestions

Contrary to myth, searing meat before it's braised doesn't seal in the juices, but it does—through a process known as the Maillard reaction—enhance the flavor of the meat through a caramelization-like process. Using beef broth (or, even better, a combination of brown stock and water) mimics that flavor and lets you skip the browning step.

Dijon Beef Roast

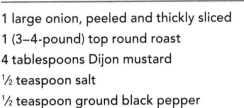

1 large onion, peeled and thickly sliced

1 (3–4-pound) top round roast

4 tablespoons Dijon mustard

1/2 teaspoon salt

1/2 teaspoon ground black pepper

1 tablespoon olive oil

1/2 cup gluten-free beef broth or water

1. Place the onion slices in a greased 4-quart slow cooker.

2. Rub the roast with the Dijon mustard. Place on top of sliced onions.

3. Sprinkle salt and pepper on top of roast and drizzle with olive oil and beef broth.

4. Cover and cook on high for 2½–3 hours or on low for 5–6 hours. Cooking time will vary depending on your preference of doneness (either rare/medium/or well done). For a rarer roast, check the internal temperature (should be around 145°F) after cooking for 1½ hours on high or 3 hours on low.

5. Serve roast with the cooked onions and au jus drizzled on top.

Pot Roast with a Touch of Sweet

1 teaspoon freshly ground black pepper

1 teaspoon smoked paprika

1 teaspoon garlic powder

1 teaspoon onion powder

½ cup lime juice

½ cup tomato sauce

1 (2-pound) chuck roast

1 large sweet onion, peeled and sliced thick

1 teaspoon coconut or olive oil

½ cup water

2 tablespoons red wine

1. In a small bowl combine the pepper, paprika, garlic powder, and onion powder.
2. In a separate bowl combine the lime juice and tomato sauce. Set aside.
3. Season all sides of the roast with the prepared spice mixture.
4. Place onion slices on the bottom of a 4-quart slow cooker.
5. Warm the oil in a large skillet over medium-high heat. Brown the roast on all sides in the skillet.
6. Place browned roast on top of the onions in the slow cooker. Turn heat to low and add water and wine to the skillet.
7. Pour pan liquid over the roast, then the lime juice and sauce mixture on top. Cover and cook on low for 8 hours.

Roast Beef for Two

½ teaspoon freshly ground black pepper

½ teaspoon fennel seeds

½ teaspoon dried rosemary

¼ teaspoon salt

½ teaspoon dried oregano

1 (¾-pound) bottom round roast, trimmed of fat

¼ cup caramelized onions

¼ cup gluten-free beef stock

1 clove garlic, peeled and sliced

1. In a small bowl stir the pepper, fennel seeds, rosemary, salt, and oregano. Rub it onto all sides of the meat. Refrigerate for 15 minutes.
2. Place the roast in a 2-quart slow cooker. Add the onions, stock, and garlic. Cook on low for 6 hours or on high for 3 hours.
3. Remove roast and slice. Serve the slices topped with the caramelized onions. Discard any cooking juices.

Red Wine Pot Roast

⅓ cup red wine

½ cup water

4 medium red potatoes, quartered

3 medium carrots, cut into thirds

2 fennel bulbs, quartered

2 medium rutabagas, peeled and quartered

1 large onion, peeled and sliced

4 cloves garlic, peeled and sliced

1 (1½-pound) lean top round roast, trimmed of fat

½ teaspoon salt

½ teaspoon freshly ground black pepper

1. Pour the wine and water into a greased 4-quart slow cooker. Add the potatoes, carrots, fennel, rutabagas, onion, and garlic. Stir.
2. Add the roast. Sprinkle with salt and pepper. Cook on low for 8 hours.
3. Remove and slice the beef. Use a slotted spoon to serve the vegetables. Discard the cooking liquid.

Easy Slow-Cooked "Roast" Beef

1 (2¼-pound) London broil roast, trimmed of fat and
   cut into pieces
Water as needed
½ teaspoon Minor's Low Sodium Beef Base
⅛ teaspoon Minor's Roasted Mirepoix Flavor Concentrate
½ tablespoon dried minced onion
½ teaspoon dried minced garlic

1. Put the roast and all other ingredients into a ceramic-lined slow cooker, add enough water to cover the roast, and set the cooker on high.

2. Once the mixture begins to boil, stir to dissolve the bases; reduce temperature to low. Allow the meat to simmer for 8 hours or until tender.

3. Remove the meat from the slow cooker and discard the resulting broth (or save it for later use). Remove any remaining fat from the meat and discard that as well. Weigh the meat and separate it into 4-ounce servings. The meat can be kept for 1–2 days in the refrigerator, or you can freeze portions for use later.

Lean Roast with Fennel and Rutabaga

1 (2-pound) boneless bottom round roast, trimmed of fat

½ teaspoon salt

½ teaspoon ground black pepper

1 large Vidalia or other sweet onion, peeled and sliced

1 (1-pound) rutabaga, peeled and cubed

2 fennel bulbs, sliced

1. Sprinkle all sides of the roast with the salt and pepper.
2. Heat a nonstick skillet for 30 seconds. Place the roast in the pan. Quickly sear each side of the roast, approximately 5 seconds per side.
3. Place the roast in a 4-quart slow cooker. Cover it with the onions, rutabaga, and fennel.
4. Cook on low for 6 hours or until desired doneness.

Slow Cooker Suggestions

Beef must reach a specific internal temperature, depending on your preference: medium rare, 145°F; medium, 160°F; and well done, 170°F. Use a probe thermometer to determine the internal temperature before you shut off the slow cooker.

Pot Roast with Root Vegetables

1 cup water

4 medium russet potatoes, scrubbed and quartered

4 medium carrots, peeled and cut into thirds

4 medium parsnips, peeled and quartered

3 medium rutabagas, peeled and quartered

2 medium onions, peeled and sliced

1 celeriac, cubed

7 cloves garlic, peeled and sliced

1 (4-pound) lean top round beef roast, excess fat removed

½ teaspoon salt

1 teaspoon paprika

½ teaspoon freshly ground black pepper

1. Pour the water into an oval 6-quart slow cooker. Add the potatoes, carrots, parsnips, rutabagas, onions, celeriac, and garlic. Stir.

2. Add the beef. Sprinkle with salt, paprika, and pepper. Cook on low for 8 hours.

3. Remove and slice the beef. Use a slotted spoon to serve the vegetables. Discard the cooking liquid.

Roast Beef

½ teaspoon freshly ground black pepper

½ teaspoon fennel seeds

½ teaspoon dried rosemary

¼ teaspoon salt

½ teaspoon dried oregano

1 (¾-pound) bottom round roast, trimmed of fat

¼ cup caramelized onions

¼ cup water or beef stock

1 clove garlic, peeled and sliced

1. In a small bowl stir the pepper, fennel seeds, rosemary, salt, and oregano. Rub it into all sides of the meat. Refrigerate for 15 minutes.

2. Place the roast in a 2-quart slow cooker. Add the onions, water or stock, and garlic. Cook on low for 8 hours. Remove and slice. Serve topped with the caramelized onions. Discard any cooking juices.

Horseradish Roast Beef and Potatoes

SERVES

6–8

⅓ cup prepared horseradish

2 tablespoons extra-virgin olive oil

1 teaspoon freshly ground black pepper

1 teaspoon dried thyme

½ teaspoon salt

1 (3-pound) boneless chuck roast, trimmed of fat and cut into 2" cubes

2 celery stalks, cut in half

¼ cup dry white wine

1¼ cups beef broth

Water

2 pounds (about 16) small red potatoes, scrubbed

1 (1-pound) package baby carrots

2 tablespoons all-purpose flour

2 tablespoons butter

1. In a small bowl mix together the horseradish, oil, pepper, thyme, and salt. Rub the horseradish mixture into meat. Add the seasoned roast, celery, white wine, and broth to a 4-quart slow cooker.

2. Cover and cook for 1–2 hours on high or until the celery is limp. Discard the celery. Add water or more broth if necessary to bring the liquid level up to just the top of the meat.

3. Add the potatoes and carrots to the cooker. Cover and cook on low for 6 hours or until meat is tender and the vegetables are cooked through. Serve warm.

4. To thicken the pan juices, remove the meat and vegetables to a serving platter. Cover and keep warm. Turn the slow cooker to high; cover and cook until the juices bubble around the edges.

5. Mix the flour together with the butter and ½ cup of the pan juices; whisk into the slow cooker. Cook, stirring constantly, for 15 minutes or until the flour taste is cooked out of the gravy and it is thickened enough to coat the back of a spoon.

Sirloin Dinner

1 (4-pound) sirloin tip roast

2 tablespoons extra-virgin olive oil

1 teaspoon plus 1/4 teaspoon kosher or sea salt, divided

1/2 teaspoon plus 1/4 teaspoon freshly ground black pepper, divided

1 teaspoon garlic powder

1 teaspoon onion powder

1 teaspoon ground cumin

1 teaspoon dried thyme

1/2 teaspoon sweet paprika

2 medium turnips, peeled and cut into 2" pieces

2 medium parsnips, peeled and cut into 2" pieces

4 large red potatoes, peeled and quartered

1 (1-pound) bag baby carrots

8 cloves garlic, peeled and cut in half lengthwise

2 large onions, peeled and sliced

1/2 cup dry red wine

1 cup beef broth

1. To ensure the roast cooks evenly, tie it into an even form using butcher's twine. Rub the oil onto the meat.

2. Mix 1 teaspoon salt, 1/2 teaspoon pepper, garlic powder, onion powder, cumin, thyme, and paprika together in a small bowl. Pat the seasoning mixture on all sides of the roast. Place the roast in the slow cooker.

3. Arrange the turnips, parsnips, potatoes, and carrots around the roast. Evenly disperse the garlic around the vegetables. Arrange the onion slices over the vegetables.

4. Pour the wine and broth into the slow cooker. Season with remaining 1/4 teaspoon salt and pepper. Cover and cook on low for 8 hours.

5. Use a slotted spoon to remove the roast and vegetables to a serving platter; cover and keep warm. Let the roast rest for at least 10 minutes before carving. To serve, thinly slice the roast across the grain. Serve drizzled with some of the pan juices.

New England Boiled Dinner

1 (3-pound) boneless beef round rump roast, cut into 8 portions

2 (10.75-ounce) cans onion soup

1 teaspoon prepared horseradish

1 bay leaf

1 clove garlic, peeled and minced

6 large carrots, peeled and cut into 1" pieces

3 medium rutabagas, peeled and quartered

4 large potatoes, peeled and quartered

1 (2-pound) head cabbage, cut into 8 wedges

2 tablespoons butter

2 tablespoons all-purpose flour

¼ teaspoon each salt and freshly ground black pepper

1 cup sour cream

1. Add the beef, soup, horseradish, bay leaf, and garlic to the slow cooker. Add the carrots, rutabagas, potatoes, and cabbage wedges. Cover and cook on low for 8 hours.

2. Remove meat and vegetables to a serving platter; cover and keep warm.

3. Increase the slow cooker setting to high; cover and cook until the pan juices begin to bubble around the edges. Mix the butter and flour in a bowl together with ½ cup of the pan juices; strain out any lumps and whisk the mixture into the simmering liquid in the slow cooker.

4. Cook and stir for 15 minutes or until the flour flavor is cooked out and the resulting gravy is thickened enough to coat the back of a spoon. Taste for seasoning and add salt and pepper if desired. Stir in the sour cream. Serve alongside or over the meat and vegetables.

Slow Cooker Suggestions

If you prefer a more intense horseradish flavor with cooked beef, increase the amount to 1 tablespoon. Taste the pan juices before you thicken it with the butter and flour mixture and add more horseradish at that time if desired. Of course, you can have some horseradish or some horseradish mayonnaise available as a condiment for those who want more.

"Corn"-It-Yourself Corned Beef, Brine Method

YIELDS

1 (3LB)

CORNED
BEEF
BRISKET

4 cups water

½ cup kosher salt

¼ cup brown sugar

1 tablespoon saltpeter

1 (3") cinnamon stick, broken in half

½ teaspoon mustard seeds

½ teaspoon black peppercorns

4 whole cloves

4 whole allspice berries

6 whole juniper berries

1 bay leaf, crumbled

¼ teaspoon ground ginger

1 pound ice

1 (3-pound) beef brisket, trimmed of fat

1 small onion, peeled and quartered

1 large carrot, peeled and sliced

1 celery stalk, diced

1. Add the water to a 4-quart or larger stockpot along with salt, brown sugar, saltpeter, cinnamon stick, mustard seeds, peppercorns, cloves, allspice berries, juniper berries, bay leaf, and ginger. Stir and cook over high heat for 10 minutes or until the salt and sugar have dissolved. Remove from the heat and add the ice. Stir until the ice has melted.

2. When the brine has cooled to 45°F, place the brisket in a 2-gallon zip-top bag or large covered container. (The container you choose needs to allow the brisket to be completely submerged in the brine.)

3. Pour in the brine. Seal or close the container, cover, and place in the refrigerator for 10 days. Daily turn the meat over in the brine, stirring the brine as you do so.

4. At the end of the 10 days, remove the meat from the brine and rinse it well under cool water.

5. Add the brisket to the slow cooker along with the onion, carrot, and celery. Add enough water to cover the meat. Cover and cook on low for 10 hours or until the meat is fork-tender. Remove the meat from the slow cooker to a cutting board; cover and allow it to rest for 30 minutes. To serve, thinly slice the brisket across the grain.

"Corn"-It-Yourself Corned Beef, Salt-Rub Method

YIELDS

1 (3LB)

CORNED BEEF BRISKET

½ cup kosher salt

1 tablespoon cracked black peppercorns

1 tablespoon dried thyme

2 teaspoons ground allspice

2 teaspoons paprika

2 bay leaves, crumbled

1 (3-pound) beef brisket, trimmed of fat

1 small onion, peeled and quartered

1 large carrot, peeled and sliced

1 celery stalk, diced

1. Add the salt, peppercorns, thyme, allspice, paprika, and bay leaves to a bowl or sandwich bag; mix well.

2. Use a fork to prick the brisket on both sides. Rub half of the salt mixture into each side of the meat. Seal in a large zip-top bag, forcing out as much air as possible. Place that bag inside of another bag. Place in the refrigerator and put a weight (such as a gallon of milk) on top. Refrigerate for 5–7 days, turning once a day.

3. At the end of the 5–7 days remove the meat from the food storage bag and rinse it well under cool water.

4. Add the brisket to the slow cooker along with the onion, carrot, and celery. Add enough water to cover the meat. Cover and cook on low for 10 hours or until the meat is fork-tender.

5. To remove more of the salt from the meat, remove it from the slow cooker and discard the cooking liquid and cooked vegetables. Place the cooked brisket back in the slow cooker and cover completely with fresh water. Cover and cook on low for 1–2 hours.

6. Remove the meat from the slow cooker to a cutting board; cover and allow it to rest for 30 minutes. To serve, thinly slice the brisket across the grain.

Kicked-Up Corned Beef and Cabbage

SERVES 6

Nonstick spray

2 medium onions, peeled and sliced

1 (3-pound) beef brisket, trimmed of fat

1 cup apple juice

¼ cup packed brown sugar

2 teaspoons finely grated orange zest

2 teaspoons prepared mustard

6 whole cloves

1 medium head cabbage, cut into 6 wedges

1. Treat the inside of the slow cooker with nonstick spray. Arrange the onion slices across the bottom of the crock. Place brisket on top of the onions.

2. Add the apple juice, brown sugar, orange zest, mustard, and cloves to a bowl and stir to mix; pour over the brisket. Cover and cook on low for 8 hours.

3. Place the cabbage on top of the brisket. Cover and cook on low for 2 more hours or until the cabbage is cooked through and the brisket is tender. Move the cabbage and meat to a serving platter. Cover and let rest for 15 minutes. Carve the brisket by slicing it against the grain.

Simple Beef and Potatoes

SERVES 6

2 pounds baby carrots, thinly sliced

1 medium onion, peeled and thinly sliced

6 medium potatoes, peeled and thinly sliced

3 celery stalks, thinly sliced

1 (3-pound) beef roast, trimmed of fat and cut into 1" cubes

3 cubes beef bouillon

½ cup water

1. Add the carrots, onion, potatoes, and celery to the slow cooker in that order. Arrange the beef cubes on top of the vegetables.

2. Dissolve the bouillon cubes in the water in a small bowl or measuring cup and pour over the beef. Cover and heat on low for 6–8 hours.

Crushed Red Pepper Beef and Pinto Beans

SERVES
6

1 pound dried pinto beans

6 cups cold water

½ pound bacon, diced

1 (1-pound) chuck roast or sirloin steak, trimmed of fat and cut into bite-sized pieces

½ teaspoon red pepper flakes

1 large onion, peeled and diced

4 cloves garlic, peeled and minced

1 (6-ounce) can tomato paste

1½ tablespoons chili powder

¼ teaspoon each salt and freshly ground black pepper

1 teaspoon ground cumin

½ teaspoon dried marjoram or cilantro

1. Rinse and drain the dried beans. Put in a bowl and add enough water to cover the beans by 2". Cover and let soak for 8 hours or overnight. Drain the beans, rinse, and add to the slow cooker along with the 6 cups water.

2. Add bacon to a nonstick skillet over medium heat. Add the steak to the skillet along with the red pepper flakes and onion; sauté for 15 minutes or until the onion is just beginning to brown.

3. Stir in the garlic and sauté for 30 seconds. Stir the sautéed mixture into the beans and water in the slow cooker. Cover and cook on low for 8 hours.

4. Stir in the tomato paste, chili powder, salt, pepper, cumin, and marjoram or cilantro. Cover and cook on low for 2 hours or until the beans are cooked through. Taste for seasoning and adjust if necessary.

Peppery Southwestern Beef

½ cup ketchup

1 tablespoon soy sauce

2 teaspoons Worcestershire sauce

1 tablespoon liquid smoke

¼ teaspoon red pepper flakes

¼ teaspoon ground nutmeg

2 teaspoons coarsely ground black pepper

2 teaspoons celery salt

¼ cup brown sugar

1 tablespoon fresh lemon juice

1 tablespoon prepared mustard

1 medium onion, peeled and chopped

1 clove garlic, peeled and minced

½ cup water

1 (4-pound) rump roast, trimmed of fat and cut
   into serving-sized pieces

1. Mix the ketchup, sauces, liquid smoke, spices, celery salt, sugar, juice, and mustard in a small bowl.
2. Mix the onion and garlic in a small bowl. Put half of the onion mixture in the bottom of the slow cooker. Add the water and sprinkle ¼ of the sauce mixture over top.
3. Arrange the meat in the slow cooker on top of the onion and sauce layers. Sprinkle the meat with half of the remaining sauce mixture.
4. Put the remaining onion mixture and sauce mixture on top of the meat.
5. Cover and heat on low for 6–8 hours.

Peking Gin Roast

1 medium onion, peeled and sliced

1 (5-pound) roast, trimmed of fat and cut into serving-sized slices

1 cup vinegar

2 tablespoons oil

2 cups black coffee

1 cup water

½ teaspoon salt

¼ teaspoon ground black pepper

½ cup gin

1. Put the onions and meat slices in a glass dish and mix; cover with the vinegar. Refrigerate for 24–48 hours, then discard the vinegar.

2. Sauté the meat and onions in oil in a large skillet over high heat until the meat is browned. Transfer the mixture to the slow cooker.

3. Pour the coffee and water over the meat and onions.

4. Cover and heat on low for 6–8 hours.

5. Half an hour before serving add the salt, pepper, and gin.

Slow Cooker Suggestions

When adapting recipes for use in a slow cooker, cut the amount of liquids in half, or more if "wet" ingredients (like tomatoes) are used. Very little evaporation takes place in a slow cooker because it is self-contained and sealed.

Beef in Beer

2 tablespoons butter

2 large onions, peeled and sliced

2 cloves garlic, peeled and minced

1 (3-pound) boneless chuck roast, trimmed of fat and cut into 6 serving-sized pieces

¼ cup water

½ cup double-strength beef broth

½ cup lager beer

1 tablespoon light brown sugar

1 tablespoon Dijon mustard

1 tablespoon apple cider vinegar

1. Melt the butter in a large nonstick skillet over medium-high heat. Add the onions and sauté for 5 minutes or until the onions are lightly browned; stir in the garlic and sauté for 30 seconds. Pour the onions and garlic into the slow cooker.

2. Put the skillet back over the heat, add the meat, and fry for 2 minutes on each side. Move the meat to the slow cooker.

3. Put the skillet back over the heat. Add the water, stirring well to bring up any browned meat clinging to the pan.

4. Stir in the broth, beer, brown sugar, mustard, and vinegar. Mix well and then pour over the meat in the slow cooker.

5. Cover and cook on low for 8 hours. Ladle onions and broth over each serving of meat.

Smothered Steak

2 medium onions, peeled and chopped

2 cloves garlic, peeled and minced

3 tablespoons flour

½ teaspoon salt

⅛ teaspoon ground black pepper

1 teaspoon dried marjoram

1 (1-pound) bottom round steak, cut across the grain into ½" × 3" strips

1 (14.5-ounce) can diced tomatoes, undrained

2 tablespoons Worcestershire sauce

1 cup beef broth

¼ cup tomato paste

1 (8-ounce) can sliced mushrooms, drained

1. Place onions and garlic in bottom of 4-quart slow cooker. Combine flour, salt, pepper, and marjoram in a large bowl. Add steak strips and toss to coat. Place steak on top of onions in slow cooker.

2. Open tomatoes and drain ¾ of can into slow cooker. Add Worcestershire sauce, beef broth, and tomato paste to remaining tomatoes in can and mix well; pour over meat. Add mushrooms.

3. Cover and cook on low for 8–10 hours until beef and vegetables are tender. Stir well and serve over hot cooked rice or noodles.

Burgundy Pepper Beef

½ cup plus 2 tablespoons flour, divided

½ teaspoon ground black pepper

2 pounds stew beef, such as blade roast or chuck steak, cubed

2 tablespoons oil

2 medium onions, peeled and quartered

½ pound mushrooms, cleaned and halved

1 tablespoon Worcestershire sauce

½ teaspoon salt

1 tablespoon sugar

1 cup water

½ cup vinegar

1 cup Burgundy wine

1. Mix ½ cup flour and pepper in a large bowl. Add the cubed beef to the flour mixture and toss to coat. Heat the meat in oil in a large skillet over medium heat until browned. Transfer the beef to the slow cooker, but keep the oil in the pan.

2. Sauté the onions and mushrooms over medium heat in the pan in the oil used for the beef until the onion mixture is soft.

3. Add the onions, mushrooms, Worcestershire sauce, salt, sugar, water, and vinegar to the slow cooker.

4. Cover and heat on low for 3–4 hours.

5. An hour before serving take 2 tablespoons of sauce from the slow cooker and let it cool briefly before mixing it well in a small bowl or mixing cup with the remaining 2 tablespoons flour. Stir this into the sauce in the slow cooker, mixing well. Add the Burgundy.

Skinny French Dip Beef for Sandwiches

1 (2-pound) lean bottom round roast, trimmed of fat and sliced into rounds

1 medium Vidalia or Walla Walla onion, peeled and sliced

2 cloves garlic, peeled and sliced

3 tablespoons soy sauce

1 tablespoon minced fresh thyme

1 teaspoon minced fresh rosemary

1 teaspoon freshly ground black pepper

1. Place beef into a 4-quart slow cooker. Add the remaining ingredients.
2. Cook for 10 hours on low or until the meat is falling apart. Shred with a fork.

French Dip Sandwiches

1 large onion, peeled, quartered, and sliced

1 (3-pound) bottom round roast, trimmed of fat

½ cup dry white wine, red wine, or water

1 envelope au jus gravy mix

⅛ teaspoon freshly ground black pepper

Hard rolls or French bread

¼ teaspoon salt

1. Line bottom of the slow cooker with the onion slices. Add the roast on top of the onion.

2. Add the wine or water, au jus mix, and pepper to a small bowl; mix well and then pour the mixture over the roast. Cook on high for 2 hours or until the meat is very tender.

3. Remove the meat from the slow cooker and let stand for 10 minutes. Cut the meat across the grain into thin slices. Serve the meat on hard rolls or French bread.

4. Taste the broth and add salt if needed. Use the broth for dipping.

Pastrami

1 (4-pound) beef brisket, trimmed of fat

2 large onions, peeled and sliced

2 cloves garlic, peeled and minced

2 tablespoons pickling spices

1½ cups water

1 tablespoon crushed black peppercorns

¾ teaspoon grated fresh nutmeg

¾ teaspoon ground allspice

2 teaspoons smoked paprika

¼ teaspoon liquid smoke

1. Add the brisket, onions, garlic, pickling spice, and water to the slow cooker. Cover and cook for 8 hours on low. Turn off the cooker and allow the meat to cool enough to handle it.
2. Preheat the oven to 350°F.
3. Add the peppercorns, nutmeg, allspice, paprika, and liquid smoke (if using) to a small bowl; mix well. Rub the peppercorn mixture over all sides of the corned beef.
4. Place on a roasting pan; roast on the middle rack for 45 minutes. Let the meat rest for 10 minutes, then carve by slicing it against the grain or on the diagonal.

Slow Cooker Suggestions

Pile thin slices of pastrami on a slice of deli rye slathered with mustard. Top with another slice of rye bread. Serve with a big, crisp kosher dill pickle.

Shredded Beef for Sandwiches

16

1 (4¼-pound) lean boneless roast, trimmed of fat

1 medium onion, peeled and chopped

3 cloves garlic, peeled and chopped

1 teaspoon paprika

1 teaspoon chili powder

½ teaspoon celery seed

½ teaspoon dried tarragon

½ teaspoon dry mustard

½ teaspoon freshly ground black pepper

¼ teaspoon salt

1 tablespoon hot sauce

1 tablespoon hickory liquid smoke

½ cup water

1. Place all ingredients into a 6–7-quart slow cooker. Cook on low for 10–12 hours. The meat should be easily shredded with a fork.

2. Remove the meat from the slow cooker to a plate. Shred with a fork. Mash the contents of the slow cooker with a potato masher. Return the beef to the slow cooker and stir to distribute the ingredients evenly.

Slow Cooker Suggestions

If the beef sitting on the shelf of the local store is too fatty, ask the butcher to cut a fresh, leaner cut. You won't have to do fat removal at home, which can be tricky depending on the cut of meat. The butcher can also suggest lean beef alternatives to fattier cuts.

Stuffed Grape Leaves

16 ounces jarred grape leaves (about 60 leaves)

Nonstick cooking spray

¾ pound 94% lean ground beef, chicken, or pork

1 medium shallot, peeled and minced

¼ cup minced dill

½ cup lemon juice, divided

2 tablespoons minced fresh parsley

1 tablespoon dried mint

1 tablespoon ground fennel

¼ teaspoon freshly ground black pepper

2 cups water

1. Prepare the grape leaves according to package instructions. Set aside.
2. Spray a medium nonstick skillet with cooking spray. Sauté the meat and shallot over medium heat until the meat is thoroughly cooked. Drain off any excess fat.
3. Scrape into a large bowl and add the dill, ¼ cup of the lemon juice, parsley, mint, fennel, and pepper. Stir to incorporate all ingredients.
4. Place a leaf stem-side up with the top of the leaf pointing away from you on a clean work surface. Place 1 teaspoon filling in the middle of the leaf. Fold the bottom toward the middle and then fold in the sides. Roll it toward the top to seal. Repeat until all leaves are used.
5. Place the rolled grape leaves in two or three layers in a 4-quart oval slow cooker. Pour in the water and remaining lemon juice. Cover and cook on low for 4–6 hours. Serve warm or cold.

Stuffed Onions

4 medium onions, peeled

1 pound ground beef or lamb

¼ teaspoon ground allspice

¼ teaspoon dried dill

3 tablespoons lemon juice, divided

2 teaspoons dried parsley

¼ teaspoon freshly ground black pepper

1 large egg

2 tablespoons almond flour

2 tablespoons extra-virgin olive oil

1 cup chicken broth

1. Cutting across the onions (not from bottom to top), cut the onions in half. Scoop out the onion cores.

2. Chop the onion cores and add to the ground beef or lamb, allspice, dill, 2 tablespoons lemon juice, parsley, pepper, and egg in a large bowl; mix well.

3. Fill the onion halves with the meat mixture. (The meat will overflow the onions and form a mound on top.) Sprinkle the almond flour over the top of the meat.

4. Add the oil to a deep 3.5-quart nonstick skillet or electric skillet over medium heat. Add the onions to the pan meat-side down and sauté for 10 minutes or until browned.

5. Arrange the onions in a 4-quart slow cooker so that the meat side is up. Mix the remaining 1 tablespoon lemon juice into the broth; pour the broth around the onions. Cover and cook on high for 4 hours or on low for 8 hours until the onion is soft and the meat is cooked through.

Slow Cooker Hamburgers

1 pound ground beef

1 large egg

2 tablespoons finely diced onion

½ teaspoon garlic powder

1 tablespoon gluten-free Worcestershire sauce

¼ teaspoon salt

¼ teaspoon ground black pepper

1. Make a 2"–3" foil rack in the bottom of your 4-quart slow cooker by placing rolled strips of aluminum foil in the bottom of the greased stoneware insert. Make a grill pattern with the strips. This will allow the burgers to cook above the juices while sitting on the rack.
2. In a medium bowl mix together all ingredients. Shape mixture into 4 flat, round burger patties.
3. Place burgers on the foil rack.
4. Cook on high for 1–1½ hours or on low for 2–2½ hours until the juices run clear when a knife or fork is inserted in the middle of each burger. Try not to overcook the burgers as they can quickly dry out.

Slow Cooker Suggestions

If you would like to make cheeseburgers, or even bacon cheeseburgers, add the cheese and precooked bacon to each patty 20 minutes prior to serving. Serve burgers on gluten-free buns, over a fresh salad, or even on top of baked French fries!

Indoor "Barbecued" Brisket Sliders

SERVES 8

Nonstick cooking spray

2 tablespoons vegetable oil

1 large onion, peeled and diced

3 cloves garlic, peeled and minced

1 (2–3-pound) beef brisket, trimmed of fat

½ cup barbecue sauce

3 tablespoons chili sauce

1 tablespoon chili powder

1 tablespoon soy sauce

1 teaspoon powdered beef bouillon

1 teaspoon ground cinnamon

1 teaspoon ground cumin

½ teaspoon ground black pepper

16 pareve dinner rolls, split horizontally

1 cup coleslaw, drained

1. Lightly spray the inside of a 6-quart slow cooker with cooking spray.

2. Heat vegetable oil in a large skillet over medium heat. Add onion and garlic and stir frequently for 3–4 minutes or until onions just start to brown. Push to the sides and add brisket.

3. Let sear for 4 minutes, then carefully use tongs to turn brisket over. Let sear for another 4 minutes.

4. Transfer brisket and onions to prepared slow cooker.

5. In a medium bowl stir together the barbecue sauce, chili sauce, chili powder, soy sauce, bouillon, cinnamon, cumin, and pepper. Pour mixture over brisket. Cover and cook on low for 7–8 hours or until brisket is very tender.

6. Transfer the brisket to a cutting board. Use two forks to shred the meat.

7. Skim any excess fat from the sauce. Return shredded meat to the cooker and stir to combine.

8. To serve, divide meat among dinner rolls. Top evenly with the drained coleslaw.

Sloppy Joes

3 pounds lean ground beef

2 tablespoons extra-virgin olive oil

1 large onion, peeled and diced

1 (15-ounce) can diced tomatoes

1 cup ketchup

¼ cup brown sugar

1 tablespoon apple cider vinegar

1 tablespoon balsamic vinegar

2 tablespoons Worcestershire sauce

1 tablespoon garlic powder

2 teaspoons chili powder

¼ teaspoon ground cinnamon

⅛ teaspoon ground cloves

¼ teaspoon each salt and freshly ground black pepper

1. Brown the ground beef in a large nonstick skillet over medium heat, breaking apart the meat as you do so. Remove and discard any fat rendered from the meat.

2. Stir in the oil and onion; sauté for 5 minutes or until the onion is transparent. Transfer the cooked ground beef and onions to the slow cooker.

3. Stir in the remaining ingredients. Cover and cook on low for 4 hours or longer.

Stromboli

½ pound thinly sliced roast beef

2 tablespoons butter

12 slices toasted French bread

½ pound thinly sliced ham

½ cup pitted and minced olives

½ pound thinly sliced mozzarella cheese

1. Sauté the beef in butter in a pan over medium heat until lightly browned.
2. Arrange the sandwich layers in this order: bread, beef, ham, olives, cheese, bread.
3. Wrap the sandwiches in foil and arrange on a trivet in the slow cooker. Pour water around the base of the trivet.
4. Cover and heat on high for 1–2 hours.

Hot Corned Beef Sandwich

2 tablespoons horseradish

½ pound cream cheese

12 slices rye bread

1 pound thinly sliced corned beef

1. Cream the horseradish and the cream cheese together in a small bowl. Arrange the sandwich layers in this order: bread, beef, cheese mixture, bread.
2. Wrap the sandwiches in foil and arrange on a trivet in the slow cooker. Pour water around the base of the trivet.
3. Cover and heat on high for 1–2 hours.

Classic Reuben

12 slices rye bread

3 tablespoons butter

1 pound thinly sliced corned beef

1 pound sauerkraut, drained until very dry

½ pound thinly sliced Swiss cheese

1 cup Russian dressing

1. Brown one side of each slice of bread in butter in a pan over medium heat.
2. Arrange the sandwich layers in this order: bread (browned-side down), beef, sauerkraut, dressing, cheese, and bread (browned-side up).
3. Wrap the sandwiches in foil and arrange on a trivet in the slow cooker. Pour water around the base of the trivet.
4. Cover and heat on high for 1–2 hours.

Slow Cooker Suggestions

Whenever possible, give your guests bite-sized food they can eat without relying on a knife. To do this, and still cut down on your prep time, use spring potatoes and baby carrots instead of large ones.

Steamers

1 clove garlic, peeled and minced

1 medium onion, peeled and minced

1 pound ground beef

1 pound pork sausage

2 large eggs

½ teaspoon salt

1 cup bread crumbs

¼ cup milk

8 hamburger buns

½ cup sliced pickles

1. In a large bowl mix the garlic, onion, meat, eggs, salt, bread crumbs, and milk.
2. Form the mixture into 8 patties.
3. Briefly sear the patties on each side in a pan over high heat. Assemble the patties on hamburger buns, with pickles on each.
4. Wrap the sandwiches in aluminum foil. Arrange the wrapped sandwiches on a trivet or rack in the slow cooker. Pour water around the base of the trivet.
5. Cover and heat on high for 1–2 hours.

Slow Cooker Suggestions

Consider every leftover for use in future cooking. Corn bread, for example, can be used in many dishes. Pop it in the freezer to use later as crumbs for meatloaf or in meatballs, giving regular old meatballs a whole new taste and texture.

CHAPTER 7

Ground Beef

Ground Beef Ragout

1 pound ground beef

2 medium onions, peeled and finely chopped

1 large green pepper, seeded and diced

1 tablespoon olive oil

1 (14.5-ounce) can Italian-style stewed tomatoes

3 medium carrots, peeled and cut into ½" slices

½ cup beef stock

½ teaspoon ground black pepper

1 medium zucchini, halved lengthwise and cut into ½" slices

1. Brown ground beef in a large skillet over medium heat, discard grease, and spoon ground beef into a greased 4-quart slow cooker.

2. In the same pan sauté the onions and green pepper in olive oil for 8–12 minutes until softened. Add onions and green pepper to slow cooker.

3. Add the tomatoes, carrots, stock, and black pepper to the slow cooker. Stir to combine all the ingredients.

4. Cook on high for 4 hours or on low for 8 hours.

5. An hour prior to serving, stir in the zucchini and allow to cook for 10–20 minutes until fork-tender.

Slow Cooker Suggestions

Instead of using zucchini, use yellow squash, precooked sweet potatoes, parsnips, or even mushrooms. Use whatever vegetables you have on hand!

Easy Italian Spaghetti

1 pound ground beef, browned

1 (16-ounce) jar marinara sauce

1 cup water

8 ounces uncooked gluten-free pasta

½ cup grated Parmesan cheese

1. Add browned ground beef, marinara sauce, and water to a greased 4-quart slow cooker. Cook on high for 2 hours or on low for 4 hours.
2. Forty-five minutes prior to serving, stir dry gluten-free pasta into meat sauce. The pasta will cook in the sauce. Serve with Parmesan cheese sprinkled on top of each serving.

Bolognese Sauce over Pasta

1 tablespoon olive oil

1 large onion, peeled and diced

1 medium carrot, peeled and chopped

2 cloves garlic, peeled and minced

1 pound ground beef

1 tablespoon minced fresh basil

1 (28-ounce) can whole tomatoes in purée

1 (28-ounce) can crushed tomatoes

1 (15-ounce) can diced tomatoes in juice

1 pound pasta, cooked

1 tablespoon chopped fresh Italian parsley (for garnish)

1. Heat the oil in a skillet on medium-high. Add the onion and carrots. Cook, stirring frequently, until the onions are softened, about 5 minutes. Add the garlic and continue to stir for 30 seconds.
2. Push the vegetable mixture to the sides and add the ground beef. Stir, breaking up the meat, until no pink remains, about 5 minutes.
3. Scrape the meat mixture into a 6-quart slow cooker. Add the remaining ingredients except the parsley. Cover and cook on low for 6–8 hours. Serve the sauce over pasta. Sprinkle with parsley if desired before serving.

One-Pot Spaghetti and Meatballs

1 slice gluten-free bread, torn in very small pieces

¼ cup 2% milk

1 pound ground beef

½ teaspoon salt

½ teaspoon ground black pepper

1½ teaspoons dried minced onion

1 large egg

1 tablespoon olive oil

1½ cups prepared spaghetti sauce

⅓ cup water

4 ounces uncooked gluten-free spaghetti, broken into small pieces

1. In a large bowl mix together bread and milk. Set aside for 5 minutes; then add ground beef, salt, pepper, dried onion, and egg. Mix well and roll into small meatballs.

2. In a medium skillet over medium heat cook the meatballs in small batches in the olive oil until they are browned, approximately 5–6 minutes. Add meatballs to a greased 2.5-quart slow cooker.

3. Add spaghetti sauce and water to the slow cooker. Cook on high for 4 hours or on low for 8 hours.

4. An hour before serving add in the spaghetti pieces and stir into the sauce. Cook spaghetti for 1 hour. Try not to overcook the pasta as it will become mushy.

Ground Beef Hash

2 pounds ground beef

2 medium onions, peeled and chopped

2 (15-ounce) cans diced tomatoes

1 large green pepper, seeded and chopped

1 cup uncooked white rice

1 tablespoon gluten-free Worcestershire sauce

2 teaspoons dried Italian seasoning

½ teaspoon salt

½ teaspoon ground black pepper

1. Brown ground beef and onions in a skillet for approximately 3–5 minutes. Pour into a greased 4-quart slow cooker. Add remaining ingredients and stir to combine.

2. Cook on high for 2–3 hours or on low for 4–6 hours until rice is cooked through.

Slow Cooker Suggestions

Whenever you purchase your groceries, go ahead and chop up several onions, peppers, carrots, potatoes, garlic, and celery. You can freeze the diced vegetables for 3–4 months in an airtight zip-top bag or store them in the refrigerator for up to a week until you need to use them.

Beef and Cabbage

1 pound cooked beef, cut into bite-sized pieces

1 small head cabbage, chopped

1 medium onion, peeled and diced

2 medium carrots, peeled and thinly sliced

2 celery stalks, sliced in ½" pieces

1 clove garlic, peeled and minced

2 cups beef broth

1 (14.5-ounce) can diced tomatoes

¼ teaspoon sugar

¼ teaspoon salt

⅛ teaspoon freshly ground black pepper

1. Add beef to the slow cooker along with the cabbage, onion, carrots, and celery; stir to mix.

2. Add the garlic, broth, tomatoes, sugar, salt, and pepper to a large bowl; mix well and pour over the beef. Set the slow cooker on high and cook for 1 hour or until the cabbage has begun to wilt.

3. Reduce heat to low and cook for 4 hours. Adjust seasonings if necessary.

Stuffed Cabbage

Water as needed

1 large head cabbage

1 teaspoon canola or flaxseed oil

½ cup sliced onions

1 (28-ounce) can whole tomatoes in purée

½ cup minced onions

1 large egg

½ tablespoon garlic powder

½ tablespoon paprika

1 pound 94% lean ground beef

1. Bring a large pot of water to boil.

2. Meanwhile, using a knife make 4 or 5 cuts around the core of the cabbage and remove the core. Discard the core and 2 layers of the outer leaves. Peel off 6–8 large whole leaves. Place the leaves in a steamer basket and allow them to steam over the boiling water for 7 minutes.

3. Allow the leaves to cool enough to handle. Dice the remaining cabbage to equal ½ cup.

4. In a large nonstick skillet over medium heat add canola or flaxseed oil. Add the sliced onions and diced cabbage and sauté for about 5 minutes until the onions are soft. Add tomatoes. Break up tomatoes into small chunks using the back of a spoon. Simmer about 10–15 minutes. Ladle ⅓ of the sauce over the bottom of a 4-quart oval slow cooker.

5. Place the minced onions, egg, garlic powder, paprika, and beef into a medium bowl. Stir to distribute all ingredients evenly.

6. Place a cabbage leaf with the open-side up and the stem part facing you on a clean work area. Add about ½ cup filling to the leaf toward the stem. Fold the sides together and then pull the top down and over the filling to form a packet. It should look like a burrito. Repeat until all the filling is gone.

7. Arrange the cabbage rolls seam-side down in a single layer in the slow cooker. Ladle about half of the remaining sauce over the rolls and repeat with a second layer. Ladle the remaining sauce over the rolls. Cover and cook on low for up to 10 hours.

Cabbage Rollatini

1 tablespoon coconut oil

½ medium onion, peeled and ground in food processor

4 cloves garlic, peeled and ground in food processor

1 teaspoon dried basil

1 teaspoon ground cumin

1 teaspoon dried oregano

½ medium head cauliflower, ground in food processor

2 pounds ground beef

½ cup almond flour

1 large egg

½ teaspoon garlic powder

1 medium head green cabbage, leaves separated and heated in microwave

1 (26-ounce) can tomato sauce

1. Heat oil in a large skillet over medium heat. Add the ground onion, ground garlic, basil, cumin, and oregano and sauté for 2–3 minutes. Remove from heat.

2. In a large bowl place the cauliflower, meat, almond flour, egg, and garlic powder. Combine thoroughly with your hands or a large spoon. Add in sautéed onion mixture and mix well.

3. Line a 4-quart slow cooker with 2 large cabbage leaves.

4. Scoop ¾ cup of the meat filling onto the stem end of the remaining cabbage leaves, and roll each cabbage leaf as tightly as possible.

5. Place rolls in slow cooker seam-side down. Pour tomato sauce evenly over top of cabbage rolls.

6. Cook on high for 4 hours. Serve warm and spoon sauce and drippings over the rolls.

Beef Barbecue

1 (3-pound) English roast
1 cup water
½ cup red wine
½ cup ketchup
1 tablespoon red wine vinegar
2 teaspoons Worcestershire sauce
2 teaspoons dry mustard
2 tablespoons dried minced onion
1 teaspoon dried minced garlic
1 teaspoon ground black pepper
1 tablespoon brown sugar
1 teaspoon chili powder
½ teaspoon ground cinnamon
¼ teaspoon ground cloves
¼ teaspoon ground ginger
Pinch ground allspice
Pinch red pepper flakes

1. Add the roast to the slow cooker. Mix all remaining ingredients together in a medium bowl and pour over the beef. Cover and cook on low for 8 hours.

2. Use a slotted spoon to remove the beef from the slow cooker; pull it apart, discarding any fat or gristle. Taste the meat and sauce and adjust seasonings if necessary.

3. To thicken the sauce, increase the heat of the cooker to high, skim any fat off the surface of the sauce (or blot it with a paper towel), and let cook uncovered while you pull apart the beef.

Slow Cooker Suggestions

Serve Beef Barbecue over your favorite cooked pasta. Top with some grated Cheddar cheese and diced sweet or green onion.

Cola-Cravin' Ground Beef

3 pounds lean ground beef

2 tablespoons extra-virgin olive oil

1 large sweet onion, peeled and diced

2 cloves garlic, peeled and minced

1 cup Coca-Cola

1 (26-ounce) jar pasta sauce

1. Brown the ground beef in a large nonstick skillet over medium heat, breaking apart the meat as you do so. Remove and discard any fat rendered from the meat.

2. Stir in the oil and onion; sauté for 5 minutes or until the onion is transparent. Stir in the garlic. Transfer the meat mixture to the slow cooker.

3. Add the cola and pasta sauce. Stir to combine. Cover and cook on low for 4 hours or longer.

Beef Burrito Filling

1 package gluten-free taco seasoning

1 clove garlic, peeled and minced

1 (2-pound) London broil roast

1 cup diced onion

2 tablespoons apple cider vinegar

1. In a small bowl mix together the taco seasoning and garlic.

2. Rub London broil with the taco seasoning mixture. Place beef and onion in a greased 4-quart slow cooker.

3. Drizzle apple cider vinegar over the meat and onions.

4. Cook on high for 4 hours or on low for 8 hours until meat can be shredded with a fork.

Taco Filling

1½ pounds 94% lean ground beef

1 medium onion, peeled and minced

1 (15-ounce) can fire-roasted diced tomatoes

1 medium Anaheim pepper, seeded and minced

2 chipotle peppers in adobo sauce, minced

½ teaspoon ground cumin

½ teaspoon ground cayenne pepper

½ teaspoon paprika

½ teaspoon garlic powder

½ teaspoon dried oregano

1. Sauté the beef and onion in a large nonstick skillet until just browned. Drain off any grease. Add to a 4-quart slow cooker. Break up any large pieces of beef with a spoon.
2. Add the remaining ingredients and stir. Cook on low for 7 hours. Stir prior to serving.

Frito Pie

3 cups lean ground beef

2 tablespoons extra-virgin olive oil

1 large white onion, peeled and diced

2½ teaspoons garlic powder

3 tablespoons chili powder

4 teaspoons ground cumin

¼ teaspoon each salt and freshly ground black pepper

2 (28-ounce) cans diced tomatoes

1 (15-ounce) can pinto beans, drained and rinsed

1 (12-ounce) bag Fritos Original Corn Chips

4 cups (1 pound) grated Cheddar cheese

½ cup diced green onions

1. Brown the ground beef in a large nonstick skillet over medium heat, breaking apart the meat as you do so. Remove and discard any fat rendered from the meat.

2. Stir in the oil and onion, garlic powder, chili powder, cumin, salt, and pepper; sauté for 5 minutes or until the onion is transparent. Transfer the ground beef mixture to the slow cooker.

3. Stir in the tomatoes and pinto beans. Cover and cook on low for 5–8 hours. (When you taste the chili for seasoning, keep in mind that it'll be served over salty corn chips.)

4. To serve, place a (1-ounce or more) handful of Fritos on each plate. Ladle the chili over the Fritos. Top with grated cheese and diced green onion if desired.

Slow Cooker Suggestions

For each serving, tear open (on the side, not the top) an individual serving–sized (1-ounce) bag of Fritos and place it flat on a serving plate. Ladle the chili into the bag and over the corn chips.

Cottage Pie with Carrots, Parsnips, and Celery

SERVES 6

1 large onion, peeled and diced

3 cloves garlic, peeled and minced

1 medium carrot, peeled and diced

1 medium parsnip, peeled and diced

1 celery stalk, diced

1 pound 94% lean ground beef

1½ cups beef stock

½ teaspoon hot paprika

½ teaspoon dried rosemary

1 tablespoon Worcestershire sauce

½ teaspoon dried savory

⅛ teaspoon salt

¼ teaspoon freshly ground black pepper

1 tablespoon cornstarch and 1 tablespoon water, mixed (if necessary)

¼ cup minced fresh parsley

2¾ cups plain mashed potatoes

1. Sauté the onions, garlic, carrots, parsnips, celery, and beef in a large nonstick skillet until the ground beef is browned. Drain off any excess fat and discard it. Place the mixture into a round 4-quart slow cooker. Add the stock, paprika, rosemary, Worcestershire sauce, savory, salt, and pepper. Stir.

2. Cook on low for 6–8 hours. If the meat mixture still looks very wet, create a slurry by mixing together 1 tablespoon cornstarch and 1 tablespoon water. Stir this into the meat mixture.

3. In a medium bowl combine the parsley and potatoes. Spread on top of the ground beef mixture in the slow cooker. Cover and cook on high for 30–60 minutes or until the potatoes are warmed through.

Slow Cooker Suggestions

Take a few minutes the night before cooking to cut up any vegetables you need for a recipe. Place them in an airtight container or plastic bag and refrigerate until morning. Measure any dried spices and place them in a small container on the counter until needed.

Steak Carnitas

1 (1½-pound) lean bottom round, trimmed of fat and cubed
3 cloves garlic, peeled and minced
1 small jalapeño, seeded and minced
¼ cup habanero salsa
¼ teaspoon salt
¼ teaspoon freshly ground black pepper
2 teaspoons ground chipotle powder
1 teaspoon New Mexican chili powder
½ teaspoon dried oregano
2 tablespoons lime juice
2 tablespoons orange juice
1 tablespoon lime zest

1. Quickly brown the beef in a large nonstick skillet over medium heat. Add to a 4-quart slow cooker.
2. In a small bowl whisk the rest of the ingredients. Pour over the beef. Stir.
3. Cook on low for 6 hours, remove the cover, and cook on high for 30 minutes. Stir before serving.

Slow Cooker Suggestions

Here are a few tips to get the most juice out of citrus. Microwave the whole fruit for 20 seconds before juicing. Roll the fruit on the countertop before you squeeze it. After squeezing the fruit the first time, use a knife to slice the membranes and squeeze it again to extract even more juice.

Chicken Stew with Meat Sauce

SERVES

4

1 pound 90% lean grass-fed ground beef

4 boneless, skinless chicken breasts

1 (6-ounce) can organic tomato paste

1 (28-ounce) can diced organic tomatoes, no salt added

4 cloves garlic, peeled and chopped

4 large carrots, peeled and sliced

2 medium red bell peppers, seeded and diced

2 medium green bell peppers, seeded and diced

1 tablespoon dried thyme

2 tablespoons olive oil

1 tablespoon chili powder

1. In a medium sauté pan over medium heat cook ground beef until browned, about 5 minutes. Drain and place in a 4–6-quart slow cooker.

2. Wipe out the sauté pan and place it over medium-high heat. Brown the chicken breasts 5 minutes per side. Add to slow cooker.

3. Combine all the remaining ingredients in the slow cooker. Cook on high for 5 hours.

4. Serve over your favorite steamed vegetable.

Soft "Shell" Beef Tacos

2 (16-ounce) jars mild or medium tomato-based salsa

2 tablespoons lime juice

5 teaspoons chili powder

1 (1½-pound) chuck roast, trimmed of fat

12 large leaves romaine lettuce (for use as taco "shells")

3 cups shredded lettuce

1 medium avocado, pitted and diced

1. Spoon 1 cup salsa into a small bowl; set aside.

2. In a 4-quart slow cooker combine remaining salsa with lime juice and chili powder.

3. Add beef, cover, and turn heat to low. Cook for 10–12 hours. Shred the meat using 2 forks and spoon into a serving bowl.

4. Lay out the romaine leaves for use as taco "shells" and place a small portion of slow-cooked beef on each.

5. Place shredded lettuce, diced avocado, and reserved salsa in small separate bowls for serving. Add toppings to tacos, wrap lettuce leaves tight, and enjoy.

CHAPTER 8

International Recipes

Americanized Moussaka

Meatless Moussaka (see recipe in this chapter)

3 pounds lean ground beef, cooked and drained of fat

1 (8-ounce) package cream cheese, cubed

1 cup heavy cream

2 large eggs

4 cups (1 pound) grated medium Cheddar cheese

1. Prepare the Meatless Moussaka recipe according to the instructions (see recipe in this chapter).

2. Stir in the cooked and drained ground beef. Stir the cream cheese cubes into the moussaka.

3. Add the heavy cream and eggs to a bowl or measuring cup; whisk until the eggs are beaten into the cream and then stir into the moussaka. Cover and cook on low for an additional 1–2 hours.

4. Gradually stir the Cheddar cheese into the mixture; cover and cook on low for 15 minutes or until the cheese is melted and can be completely stirred into the moussaka. If you won't be serving the moussaka immediately, reduce the heat on the slow cooker to warm.

Meatless Moussaka

¾ cup dry brown or yellow lentils, rinsed and drained

2 large potatoes, peeled and diced

1 cup water

1 celery stalk, finely diced

1 medium sweet onion, peeled and diced

3 cloves garlic, peeled and minced

½ teaspoon salt

¼ teaspoon ground cinnamon

Pinch freshly ground nutmeg

¼ teaspoon freshly ground black pepper

¼ teaspoon dried basil

¼ teaspoon dried oregano

¼ teaspoon dried parsley

1 medium eggplant, diced

12 baby carrots, each cut into 3 pieces

1 (14.5-ounce) can diced tomatoes, undrained

1 (8-ounce) package cream cheese, softened

2 large eggs

1. Add the lentils, potatoes, water, celery, onion, garlic, salt, cinnamon, nutmeg, pepper, basil, oregano, and parsley to the slow cooker; stir. Top with eggplant and carrots. Cover and cook on low for 6 hours or until the lentils are cooked through.

2. Stir in undrained tomatoes. Mix cream cheese and eggs together in a small bowl; dollop over lentil mixture. Cover and cook on low for an additional ½ hour.

Slimmed-Down Moussaka

2 (1-pound) eggplants, peeled

2 teaspoons salt

1 teaspoon olive oil

1 large onion, peeled and diced

2 cloves garlic, peeled and minced

1 (20-ounce) can whole tomatoes in purée

1 tablespoon tomato paste

½ teaspoon ground cinnamon

1 tablespoon minced fresh oregano

1 tablespoon minced fresh flat-leaf parsley

1 pound 94% lean ground beef

1 cup fat-free evaporated milk

1 tablespoon butter

1 large egg

2 tablespoons flour

1. Slice the eggplants vertically into ¼"-thick slices. Place in a colander and lightly salt the eggplant. Allow to drain for 15 minutes. Meanwhile, preheat the oven to 375°F. Rinse off the eggplant slices and pat them dry. Arrange the slices in a single layer on two parchment paper–lined baking sheets. Bake for 15 minutes.

2. While prepping the eggplant, heat the oil in a large nonstick skillet. Sauté the onion and garlic for 1 minute, then add the tomatoes, tomato paste, cinnamon, oregano, parsley, and ground beef. Break up the tomatoes into small chunks using the back of a spoon.

3. Simmer, stirring occasionally, until the meat is browned and most of the liquid evaporates.

4. Ladle half of the sauce onto the bottom of a 4- or 6-quart oval slow cooker. Top with a single layer of eggplant, taking care to leave no gaps between slices. Top with remaining sauce. Top with another layer of eggplant. Cover with the lid and cook for 2½–3 hours on high or up to 6 hours on low.

5. In a small saucepan whisk together the evaporated milk, butter, egg, and flour. Bring to a boil and then reduce the heat. Whisk until smooth.

6. Pour the sauce over the eggplant and cook an additional 1–1½ hours on high.

Beef Bourguignon

8 slices bacon, diced

1 large yellow onion, peeled and diced

3 cloves garlic, peeled and minced

1 (3-pound) boneless English or chuck roast, trimmed of fat and cut into bite-sized pieces

16 ounces fresh mushrooms, cleaned and sliced

2 tablespoons tomato paste

2 cups beef broth or water

4 cups Burgundy wine

½ teaspoon dried thyme

1 bay leaf

¼ teaspoon each salt and freshly ground black pepper

1 large yellow onion, peeled and thinly sliced

½ cup butter, softened

½ cup all-purpose flour

1. Add the bacon to a large nonstick skillet; fry the bacon over medium heat until it renders its fat. Use a slotted spoon to remove the bacon and reserve it for another use or use it in a tossed salad to accompany the meal.

2. Add the onion to the skillet and sauté for 5 minutes or until the onion is transparent. Stir in the garlic, sauté for 30 seconds, and then transfer the onion mixture to the slow cooker. Cover the cooker.

3. Add the beef pieces to the skillet and brown the meat over medium-high heat for 5 minutes. Transfer the meat to the slow cooker. Cover the cooker. Add half of the sliced mushrooms to the skillet; stir-fry for 5 minutes or until the mushroom liquids have evaporated; transfer to the slow cooker and replace the cover.

4. Add the tomato paste to the skillet and sauté for 3 minutes or until the tomato paste just begins to brown. Stir in the broth or water, scraping the bottom of the pan to remove any browned bits and work them into the sauce.

5. Remove the pan from the heat and stir in the Burgundy, thyme, bay leaf, salt, and pepper; stir to combine. Pour into the slow cooker. Add the remaining mushrooms and sliced onion to the slow cooker. Cover and cook on low for 8 hours.

continued on next page

6. To thicken the sauce use a slotted spoon to transfer the meat and much of the cooked onions and mushrooms to a serving platter; cover and keep warm.

7. In a small bowl or measuring cup mix the butter together with the flour to form a paste; whisk in some of the pan liquid a little at a time to thin the paste. Strain out any lumps if necessary. Increase the heat of the cooker to high.

8. When the pan liquids begin to bubble around the edges, whisk in the flour mixture. Cook, stirring constantly, for 15 minutes or until the flour taste is cooked out of the sauce and it has thickened enough to coat the back of a spoon. Taste for seasoning and add additional salt and pepper if needed. Pour over the meat, mushrooms, and onions on the serving platter.

Slow Cooker Suggestions

You can steam potatoes for the Beef Bourguignon if you rest 8 medium peeled red potatoes on top of the beef liquid in the slow cooker; remove them to the serving platter after you complete Step 4.

Borscht

1½ tablespoons extra-virgin olive oil

1 clove garlic, peeled and minced

1 (½-pound) chuck roast, cut into ½" pieces

1 small yellow onion, peeled and diced

1 pound red beetroots with greens

1 small head cabbage, cored and chopped

1 (15-ounce) can diced tomatoes

7 cups beef broth

¼ cup red wine vinegar

2 bay leaves

1 tablespoon lemon juice

¼ teaspoon each salt and freshly ground black pepper

½ cup sour cream (for garnish)

Fresh chopped dill (for garnish)

1. Add the oil, garlic, beef, and onion to the slow cooker; stir to coat the beef and vegetables in the oil. Cover and cook on high for 30 minutes or until the onion is transparent.

2. Peel and dice the beets. (You may wish to wear gloves; beet juice can stain your hands and fingernails. Be careful, because it can also stain some countertops.) Reserve the beet greens; rinse well and cover them with cold water until needed.

3. Add the cabbage, tomatoes, beets, beef broth, vinegar, bay leaves, and lemon juice to the slow cooker. Cover and cook on low for 7 hours.

4. Chop the reserved beet greens and add to the soup; cover and cook on low for another 15 minutes or until the greens are wilted. Taste for seasoning and add salt and pepper if desired. Ladle the soup into bowls and garnish each bowl with a heaping tablespoon of sour cream and some fresh dill.

Winter Borscht

1 (¾-pound) lean top round, cubed

3½ cups shredded cooked beets

1 medium onion, peeled and diced

1 medium carrot, peeled and grated

½ teaspoon salt

½ teaspoon sugar

3 tablespoons red wine vinegar

½ teaspoon freshly ground black pepper

½ tablespoon dill seed

1 clove garlic, peeled and minced

1 cup shredded green cabbage

2 cups vegetable stock or beef broth

2 cups water

1. In a large nonstick skillet sauté the beef for 1 minute. Drain off any excess fat.

2. Place the beef and the remaining ingredients into a 4-quart slow cooker. Cook on low for 8 hours. Stir before serving.

Iranian Beef Roast

2 celery stalks, diced

1 (3-pound) boneless chuck roast

¼ teaspoon salt

2 large onions, peeled and quartered

2 cloves garlic, peeled and minced

2 cups beef broth

¼ cup red wine vinegar

2 (15-ounce) cans diced tomatoes

1 tablespoon dried cilantro

¾ teaspoon freshly ground black pepper

¾ teaspoon ground cumin

½ teaspoon ground coriander

¼ teaspoon ground cloves

⅛ teaspoon ground cardamom

⅛ teaspoon ground nutmeg

⅛ teaspoon ground cinnamon

8 medium red potatoes

1 (16-ounce) bag frozen cut green beans, thawed

¼ cup butter, softened

¼ cup all-purpose flour

1. Add the celery, roast, salt, onion, garlic, broth, vinegar, diced tomatoes, cilantro, pepper, cumin, coriander, cloves, cardamom, nutmeg, and cinnamon to the slow cooker.

2. Wash and cut a strip around each potato. Add to the slow cooker on top of the other ingredients. Cover and cook on low for 6 hours.

3. Add the green beans to the slow cooker. Cover and cook an additional 30 minutes on low or until the green beans are heated through.

continued on next page

4. If you wish to thicken the pan juices to make gravy, use a slotted spoon to transfer the meat and vegetables to a serving platter; cover and keep warm.

5. Strain the broth remaining in the pan and then return 1½ cups of the strained pan juices to the slow cooker. Increase the temperature on the slow cooker to high; cover and cook for 15 minutes or until the juices are bubbling around the edges.

6. In a small bowl use a fork to blend together the butter and flour. Whisk the butter-flour mixture into the boiling juices a teaspoon at a time.

7. Once you've added all of the mixture, continue to cook and stir for 10 minutes or until the flour taste is cooked out of the gravy and it is thickened enough to coat the back of a spoon. Taste for seasoning and add additional salt and pepper if desired.

Slow Cooker Suggestions

Instead of adding green beans to the slow cooker, you can steam them and serve warm dressed with your favorite vinaigrette. Season with salt and pepper to taste.

Beef Rogan Josh

1 (1-pound) bottom round, trimmed of fat and cubed

1 medium onion, peeled and diced

4 cloves garlic, peeled and minced

2 tablespoons ground cumin

2 tablespoons ground coriander

1 tablespoon ground turmeric

2 teaspoons ground cardamom

2 teaspoons minced fresh ginger

2 teaspoons freshly ground black pepper

2 teaspoons chili powder

1 (28-ounce) can crushed tomatoes

1 cup fat-free Greek yogurt

1. In a large nonstick skillet sauté the beef, onion, and garlic until just browned. Drain off any excess fat. Place into a 4-quart slow cooker.
2. Add the spices and crushed tomatoes. Cook on low for 8 hours. Stir in the yogurt prior to serving.

Cuban Picadillo

½ pound 94% lean ground beef

¼ cup diced tomato

¼ cup pimento-stuffed green olives

½ tablespoon nonpareil capers

1 medium shallot, peeled and minced

½ tablespoon tomato paste

¼ teaspoon ground cumin

⅛ teaspoon freshly ground black pepper

⅛ teaspoon salt

1. In a small nonstick skillet sauté the beef until cooked through. Break up large pieces with the back of a spoon.

2. Add the meat and remaining ingredients to a 2-quart slow cooker. Stir to distribute all ingredients evenly. Cook on low for 6–8 hours. Stir prior to serving.

Slow Cooker Suggestions

Freshly ground pepper has a fresher, spicier flavor than ground pepper. To keep it free flowing, ground pepper is often packaged with fillers that can dull the flavor. Whole peppercorns take just seconds to grind in a peppermill.

Ropa Vieja

1 (2-pound) top round roast

1 medium cubanelle pepper, seeded and diced

1 large onion, peeled and diced

2 medium carrots, peeled and diced

1 (28-ounce) can crushed tomatoes

2 cloves garlic, peeled

1 tablespoon dried oregano

$\frac{1}{2}$ teaspoon ground cumin

$\frac{1}{2}$ cup sliced pimento-stuffed green olives

1. Place the roast, pepper, onions, carrots, tomatoes, garlic, oregano, and cumin into a 2-quart slow cooker. Cook on high for 7 hours. Add the olives and continue to cook for 20 minutes.

2. Shred the meat with a fork, then mash it with a potato masher until very well mixed.

Rouladen

¼ cup red wine

1 cup water

4 very thin round steaks (about ¾ pound total)

2 tablespoons grainy German-style mustard

1 tablespoon lean bacon crumbles

4 dill pickle spears

1. Pour the wine and water into the bottom of an oval 4-quart slow cooker.

2. Place the steaks horizontally on a platter. Spread ½ tablespoon mustard on each steak and sprinkle with ¼ of the bacon crumbles. Place one of the pickle spears on one end of each steak.

3. Roll each steak toward the other end, so it looks like a spiral. Place on a large skillet over medium heat seam-side down. Cook for 1 minute, then use tongs to flip the steaks carefully and cook the other side for 1 minute.

4. Place each roll in a single layer in the water-wine mixture. Cook on low for 1 hour. Remove the rolls, discarding the cooking liquid.

Slow Cooker Suggestions

Roulade, the generic term for steak wrapped around a savory filling, works best with steaks that are approximately ⅛" thick, 8"–10" long, and 5" wide. Look for them in the meat section labeled as "rolling steaks," or ask the butcher to specially cut some. They are a great way to enjoy red meat in small portions.

Sauerbraten

1 teaspoon whole allspice berries

1 teaspoon mustard seeds

2 tablespoons black peppercorns

1 bay leaf

3 whole cloves

1¾ cups red wine vinegar

½ cup apple cider vinegar

1 teaspoon salt

1 tablespoon sugar

1 (3½-pound) top round roast

2 medium onions, peeled and sliced

2 medium carrots, peeled and sliced

6 reduced-fat gingersnap cookies

1. Place the allspice, mustard seeds, peppercorns, bay leaf, and cloves in cheesecloth. Tie it closed with kitchen twine. Place it into a large resealable plastic bag. Add the vinegars, salt, sugar, and meat. Marinate overnight.

2. The next day place the entire contents of the bag along with the onions and carrots into a 4-quart slow cooker. Cook on low for 8–10 hours. During the last 30 minutes of cooking time skim off any visible fat that may have risen to the top. Remove the bag of spices, add the gingersnaps, and turn the heat to high.

3. Thirty minutes after the gingersnaps have been added, break the meat into chunks using a serving spoon. Serve hot with dumplings on the side.

Slow Cooker Suggestions

Potato dumplings make a great accompaniment to Sauerbraten. To make dumplings: In a large bowl mix 4 cups plain mashed potatoes, 3 cups flour, ¾ teaspoon baking powder, 1 egg, and a pinch salt until a dough forms. Bring a large pot of water to a boil and add ice-cream scoops of dough to the water. Boil until they float to the top, about 5 minutes.

Greek Meatballs

1½ pounds lean ground beef

1 cup converted rice

1 small yellow onion, peeled and finely diced

3 cloves garlic, peeled and minced

2 teaspoons dried parsley

½ teaspoon dried oregano

1 teaspoon ground cumin

2 teaspoons dried mint

1 large egg

All-purpose flour

2 cups tomato juice or tomato-vegetable juice

2 tablespoons Greek extra-virgin olive oil

½ teaspoon ground cinnamon

1 tablespoon honey

4 cups water

¼ teaspoon each salt and freshly ground black pepper

1. Make the meatballs by mixing the ground beef together with the rice, onion, garlic, parsley, oregano, cumin, mint, and egg in a large bowl; shape into small meatballs and roll each one in flour.

2. Add the tomato or tomato-vegetable juice, olive oil, cinnamon, and honey to the slow cooker. Carefully add the meatballs. Pour in the water. (The water should take the liquid level up to where it completely covers the meatballs.)

3. Cover and cook on low for 6 hours or until the meatballs are cooked through. Taste for seasoning and add salt and pepper if needed.

Italian Meatballs

4 tablespoons extra-virgin or light olive oil

1 large sweet onion, peeled and diced

4 cloves garlic, peeled and minced, divided

2 (28-ounce) cans plum tomatoes, drained and chopped

1 (6-ounce) can tomato paste

1 cup chicken broth

½ teaspoon sugar

Pinch red pepper flakes

1 pound lean ground beef

½ pound ground veal

½ pound lean ground pork

⅓ cup bread crumbs

¼ cup freshly grated Parmigiano-Reggiano or Romano cheese

6 tablespoons minced fresh Italian parsley

¼ teaspoon each salt and freshly ground black pepper

1. Add the oil and onion to the slow cooker; stir to coat the onions in the oil. Cover and cook on high for 30 minutes or until the onion is transparent. Stir in half of the minced garlic, tomatoes, tomato paste, broth, sugar, and red pepper flakes. Cover and cook on high while you make the meatballs.

2. Add the remaining half of minced garlic, beef, veal, pork, bread crumbs, cheese, parsley, salt, and pepper to a large bowl; use your hands to mix.

3. Shape into 16 equal-sized meatballs. Add the meatballs to the slow cooker. Reduce the temperature of the slow cooker to low; cover and cook for 7 hours or until the internal temperature of the meatballs is 160°F.

Slow Cooker Suggestions

Some fat will be rendered from the Italian meatballs during the slow-cooking process. It will rise to the surface, so skim it from the sauce and discard. Carefully ladle the meatballs from the slow cooker before you whisk the sauce to evenly distribute the onions and other ingredients, or use an immersion blender if you prefer a smoother sauce.

Portuguese Beef Stew

2 tablespoons extra-virgin olive oil

1 (3-pound) bottom round, trimmed of fat and cut into bite-sized pieces

¼ teaspoon each salt and freshly ground black pepper

1 large onion, peeled and diced

2 cloves garlic, peeled and minced

1 cup Zinfandel or other dry red wine

1 (6-ounce) can tomato paste

1 (28-ounce) can diced tomatoes, undrained

1 cup beef broth

1½ tablespoons pickling spices

1 bay leaf

2 teaspoons dried mint

1. Add the oil to the slow cooker. Add the meat to the cooker along with the salt, pepper, onion, and garlic. Stir to coat the meat and vegetables in the oil.

2. Add the wine, tomato paste, tomatoes, and broth to a medium bowl or large measuring cup. Stir to mix. Pour into the slow cooker. Add the pickling spices and bay leaf.

3. Cover and cook on low for 7 hours or until the beef is cooked through and tender. Skim and discard any fat from the surface of the stew in the slow cooker. Remove and discard the bay leaf.

4. Stir in the dried mint; cover and continue to cook on low for 15 minutes to allow the mint to blend into the stew. (If you have fresh mint available, you can instead sprinkle about 1 teaspoon of minced fresh mint over each serving. Garnish each serving with a sprig of mint as well if desired.)

Slow Cooker Suggestions

When pickling spices are used in a dish, they're usually added to a muslin cooking bag or a tea ball or tied into a piece of cheesecloth. After the cooking time, they're pulled from the pot and discarded. For this Portuguese Beef Stew recipe you can simply stir them in with the other ingredients.

Braciole

½ teaspoon olive oil

½ cup diced onions

2 cloves garlic, peeled and minced

1 (32-ounce) can diced tomatoes

8 rapini stalks

8 very thin-cut round steaks (about 1¼ pounds total)

4 teaspoons bread crumbs

4 teaspoons grated Parmesan cheese

1. Heat the oil in a nonstick pan. Sauté the onions and garlic until the onions are soft, about 5 minutes. Place in a 6-quart oval slow cooker. Add the tomatoes and stir.

2. Cut the stems off the rapini. Place the steaks on a platter horizontally. Sprinkle each steak with ½ teaspoon bread crumbs and ½ teaspoon Parmesan.

3. Place a bunch of rapini leaves on one end of each steak. Roll each steak toward the other end. It should look like a spiral.

4. Place in the skillet seam-side down and cook on medium heat for 1 minute. Use tongs to flip the steaks carefully and cook the other side for 1 minute.

5. Place each roll in a single layer on top of the tomato sauce. Cover and cook on low for 1–2 hours or until the steaks are cooked through.

Shortcut Albondigas Soup

5 cups gluten-free beef broth

2 large carrots, peeled and diced

$\frac{1}{3}$ cup uncooked white rice

1 medium onion, peeled and diced

1$\frac{1}{2}$ cups medium-hot salsa

2 slices gluten-free bread, crumbled

$\frac{1}{2}$ cup milk

1$\frac{1}{2}$ pounds ground beef

2 teaspoons dried mint

$\frac{1}{2}$ teaspoon salt

$\frac{1}{2}$ teaspoon ground black pepper

1. Grease a 4–6-quart slow cooker. Add broth, carrots, rice, onion, and salsa.
2. In a medium bowl combine crumbled gluten-free bread with milk and mix until bread is softened. Stir in ground beef, mint, salt, and pepper.
3. Form 1"–2" meatballs with your hands and drop them in the soup. Cover and cook on high for 4 hours or on low for 8 hours.

Slow Cooker Suggestions

The flavor of these meatballs is distinctive because of the mint used. Some people also add additional mint into the soup itself because they enjoy the flavor so much. If you cannot find dried mint in the spices section of your grocery store, simply use a few teaspoons of dried mint from an herbal teabag. Alternatively, if your family isn't a fan of mint, use freshly chopped cilantro instead.

Asian Pepper Steak

SERVES
4

2 tablespoons coconut oil

2 pounds sirloin steak or any other good cut, sliced on an angle into ½" strips

¼ teaspoon ground black pepper

2 cloves garlic, peeled and minced

¼ cup wheat-free tamari

1 (16-ounce) can diced tomatoes

1 large green pepper, seeded and sliced in thin strips

1 small onion, peeled and sliced

1. In a large frying pan add the oil and heat over medium heat. Sauté the steak for 10–15 minutes until it lightly browns.

2. Drain excess fat, liberally coat the meat with black pepper, and put the meat in a 4- or 6-quart slow cooker.

3. Add garlic and tamari and mix so that the steak is thoroughly coated. Cook on low for 6 hours.

4. One hour before serving add tomatoes, green peppers, and onions; turn the slow cooker to high. Cook for 1 hour and then serve piping hot.

Beef and Coconut Curry

2 tablespoons canola oil

1 (2-pound) chuck roast, trimmed of fat and
cut into 2" pieces

2 large onions, peeled and each cut into 8 wedges

4 cloves garlic, peeled and finely chopped

2 tablespoons finely chopped fresh ginger

12 ounces coconut milk

2 tablespoons honey

1 tablespoon curry powder

1 teaspoon ground cayenne pepper

1 pint cherry tomatoes

1. In a large skillet warm oil over medium-high heat. Brown beef on all
   sides. Transfer to a 4-quart slow cooker along with onions, garlic, and
   ginger.

2. In a large bowl whisk together the coconut milk, honey, curry powder,
   and cayenne pepper and pour over meat. Cover and cook on low
   until meat is fork-tender, about 4–5 hours.

3. Stir in cherry tomatoes and let them warm and soften in stew for
   15–20 minutes.

Beef and Ginger Curry

1 pound stewing steak cubes

1 tablespoon olive oil

¼ teaspoon ground black pepper

2 cloves garlic, peeled and minced

1 teaspoon chopped fresh ginger

1 small fresh green chili, seeded and diced

1 tablespoon curry powder

1 (14-ounce) can stewed tomatoes, chopped

1 large onion, peeled and quartered

8 ounces beef stock

1. In a large frying pan brown the steak in the olive oil for 5–10 minutes. Once browned remove from pan, leaving juices. Season beef with pepper.
2. In the remaining juice from the steak, cook the garlic, ginger, and chili in the frying pan for 2 minutes, stirring frequently.
3. Season with curry powder. Mix in the chopped tomatoes.
4. Place the onion on bottom of a 2- or 4-quart slow cooker; layer the browned beef over top.
5. Add mixture from pan to the slow cooker and add the beef stock. Cover and cook on low for 6–8 hours.

Tzimmes

1 (3-pound) beef brisket

1 large yellow onion, peeled and diced

¼ teaspoon each salt and freshly ground black pepper

2 celery stalks, diced

1 large carrot, peeled and diced

1 (12-ounce) box pitted prunes (dried plums)

1 tablespoon dried or freeze-dried parsley

3 cups beef broth

3 tablespoons fresh lemon juice

¼ teaspoon ground cloves

1 teaspoon ground cinnamon

1 tablespoon honey

2 tablespoons white wine or white wine vinegar

4 large sweet potatoes, peeled and quartered

2 tablespoons butter

1. Add the brisket, onion, salt, pepper, celery, carrot, prunes, and parsley to the slow cooker.

2. Mix the broth, lemon juice, cloves, cinnamon, honey, and vinegar together in a medium bowl and pour over the meat. Cover and cook on low for 6 hours or until the meat is cooked through.

3. Add the sweet potatoes. Cover and cook on low for another 2 hours or until the brisket and sweet potatoes are tender. Use a slotted spoon to move the vegetables and meat to a serving platter. Tent with foil or otherwise cover and keep warm.

4. Allow the meat to rest for 15 minutes before you carve it, slicing it against the grain.

5. For a richer sauce, after you remove the meat and vegetables to a serving platter whisk the butter into the pan juices a teaspoon at a time before spooning it over the dish.

Beef Biryani

1 (1-pound) top round, cut into strips

1 tablespoon minced fresh ginger

½ teaspoon ground cloves

½ teaspoon ground cardamom

½ teaspoon ground coriander

½ teaspoon freshly ground black pepper

½ teaspoon ground cinnamon

½ teaspoon ground cumin

¼ teaspoon salt

2 cloves garlic, peeled and minced

1 medium onion, peeled and minced

1 cup fat-free Greek yogurt

1 cup frozen peas

1½ cups cooked basmati or brown rice

1. Place the beef, spices, garlic, and onion into a 4-quart slow cooker. Stir. Cook on low for 7–8 hours.

2. About 30 minutes before serving stir in the yogurt, peas, and rice. Cook for 30 minutes. Stir before serving.

Irish Boiled Dinner

2 tablespoons extra-virgin olive oil

1 tablespoon butter, melted

2 cups leeks, white part only, chopped and rinsed

1 large yellow onion, peeled and sliced

3 cloves garlic, peeled and minced

1 (3½-pound) beef brisket

2 bay leaves

10 black peppercorns

½ cup chopped fresh parsley

2 teaspoons salt

1 (1-pound) bag baby carrots

16 small red potatoes

2 medium turnips, peeled and quartered

1 (12-ounce) bottle lager-type beer

1 cup beef broth

2 small heads cabbage, cored and cut into wedges

¼ teaspoon each salt and freshly ground black pepper

1. Add the oil and butter to the slow cooker along with the leeks and onion; stir to coat the vegetables in oil. Cover and cook on high for 30 minutes or until the leeks and onions are soft and transparent. Stir in the garlic.

2. Add the brisket to the slow cooker along with the bay leaves, peppercorns, parsley, salt, carrots, potatoes, turnips, beer, and broth; cover, reduce the temperature of the slow cooker to low, and cook for 7 hours.

3. Add the cabbage wedges, pressing them down into the liquid; cover and cook for an additional 30–60 minutes or until all vegetables are cooked according to your preference. Taste for seasoning and add additional salt and pepper if needed.

Beef Cholent

½ cup lima beans

½ cup navy beans

1 cup pearl barley

1 small onion, peeled and chopped

1 medium carrot, peeled and cut into 1" pieces

1 pound beef flanken ribs

2 medium or large potatoes, peeled and cut into large chunks

1 teaspoon sweet paprika

1 teaspoon garlic powder

4 cups water plus more if needed

2 teaspoons kosher salt

½ teaspoon ground black pepper

1. Place lima beans, navy beans, and barley in a fine mesh drainer. Rinse several times in cold water and drain.

2. In a 6-quart slow cooker place ingredients in the following order: chopped onion, carrot, flanken, prepared beans and barley, potatoes, paprika, garlic powder, and water.

3. Cover and cook on low for 12–26 hours. Check and add water at any time if cholent looks too dry. If there is too much liquid at the end of the cooking time, uncover and let cook for an additional 30 minutes. Add salt and pepper. Taste and add additional salt and pepper if needed.

Slow Cooker Suggestions

Cholent (CHUH-lent) is a stew traditionally assembled and set over a low flame just before Shabbat begins at sundown Friday night and left to cook overnight and on through the entire next day until after sundown, when Shabbat is over. Since work (which includes lighting a flame or turning on an oven) is prohibited during this seventh day of rest, this dish allows observant Jews to have a warm meal on Saturday night at a reasonable hour.

Sephardic Cholent

Nonstick cooking spray

2 tablespoons olive oil

2 large onions, peeled and chopped

4 cloves garlic, peeled and coarsely chopped

3 pounds beef flanken ribs

2 (15-ounce) cans chickpeas, drained and rinsed

3 large sweet potatoes, peeled and cut into 1" chunks

2 teaspoons ground cumin

1 teaspoon ground turmeric

1 teaspoon ground cinnamon

1 tablespoon paprika

½ teaspoon kosher salt

¼ teaspoon ground black pepper

3 tablespoons honey

Pinch crushed saffron threads

1 cup chicken broth

6 uncooked whole eggs

1. Spray the inside of a 6-quart slow cooker with the cooking spray.

2. Heat oil in a large skillet over medium-high heat. Add onions and cook, stirring frequently, until they soften and just start to turn brown, about 8 minutes.

3. Add garlic; stir for 30 seconds, then push mixture to the sides. Add flanken and let sear for 3 minutes without disturbing. Carefully turn flanken and sear again for 3 minutes.

4. Transfer flanken and onions into prepared slow cooker and top with chickpeas and sweet potatoes. Sprinkle in the cumin, turmeric, cinnamon, paprika, salt, and pepper. Drizzle in the honey.

5. In a small bowl mix the saffron into the broth and pour into slow cooker.

6. Nestle the eggs in the center of the slow cooker. Cover and cook on low for 8–12 hours.

Better-Than-Takeout Mongolian Beef

1 (3-pound) lean chuck roast, trimmed of fat

3 cloves garlic, peeled and grated

1 knob peeled fresh gingerroot, grated, or 1 teaspoon ground ginger

1 medium onion, peeled and thinly sliced

½ cup water

½ cup low-sodium soy sauce

2 tablespoons balsamic vinegar

2 tablespoons hoisin sauce

1 tablespoon five-spice powder

1 tablespoon cornstarch

1 teaspoon red pepper flakes

1 teaspoon sesame oil

1. Place all ingredients in a 4-quart slow cooker. Cover and cook for 5 hours on low or until the meat is thoroughly cooked through and tender.

2. Remove the roast to a cutting board. Slice thinly and return it to the slow cooker. Cook for an additional 20 minutes on high. Stir the meat and the sauce before serving.

US/Metric Conversion Chart

VOLUME CONVERSIONS

US Volume Measure	Metric Equivalent
⅛ teaspoon	0.5 milliliter
¼ teaspoon	1 milliliter
½ teaspoon	2 milliliters
1 teaspoon	5 milliliters
½ tablespoon	7 milliliters
1 tablespoon (3 teaspoons)	15 milliliters
2 tablespoons (1 fluid ounce)	30 milliliters
¼ cup (4 tablespoons)	60 milliliters
⅓ cup	90 milliliters
½ cup (4 fluid ounces)	125 milliliters
⅔ cup	160 milliliters
¾ cup (6 fluid ounces)	180 milliliters
1 cup (16 tablespoons)	250 milliliters
1 pint (2 cups)	500 milliliters
1 quart (4 cups)	1 liter (about)

WEIGHT CONVERSIONS

US Weight Measure	Metric Equivalent
½ ounce	15 grams
1 ounce	30 grams
2 ounces	60 grams
3 ounces	85 grams
¼ pound (4 ounces)	115 grams
½ pound (8 ounces)	225 grams
¾ pound (12 ounces)	340 grams
1 pound (16 ounces)	454 grams

OVEN TEMPERATURE CONVERSIONS

Degrees Fahrenheit	Degrees Celsius
200 degrees F	95 degrees C
250 degrees F	120 degrees C
275 degrees F	135 degrees C
300 degrees F	150 degrees C
325 degrees F	160 degrees C
350 degrees F	180 degrees C
375 degrees F	190 degrees C
400 degrees F	205 degrees C
425 degrees F	220 degrees C
450 degrees F	230 degrees C

BAKING PAN SIZES

American	Metric
8 x 1½ inch round baking pan	20 x 4 cm cake tin
9 x 1½ inch round baking pan	23 x 3.5 cm cake tin
11 x 7 x 1½ inch baking pan	28 x 18 x 4 cm baking tin
13 x 9 x 2 inch baking pan	30 x 20 x 5 cm baking tin
2 quart rectangular baking dish	30 x 20 x 3 cm baking tin
15 x 10 x 2 inch baking pan	30 x 25 x 2 cm baking tin (Swiss roll tin)
9 inch pie plate	22 x 4 or 23 x 4 cm pie plate
7 or 8 inch springform pan	18 or 20 cm springform or loose bottom cake tin
9 x 5 x 3 inch loaf pan	23 x 13 x 7 cm or 2 lb narrow loaf or pate tin
1½ quart casserole	1.5 liter casserole
2 quart casserole	2 liter casserole

INDEX

170 Slow Cooker Favorites: Beef